SAVAGE GRACE

SAVAGE GRACE

LIVING RESILIENTLY IN THE DARK NIGHT OF THE GLOBE

By Andrew Harvey and Carolyn Baker

SAVAGE GRACE
LIVING RESILIENTLY IN THE DARK
NIGHT OF THE GLOBE

iUniverse books may be ordered through booksellers or by contacting:

iUniverse
1663 Liberty Drive
Bloomington, IN 47403
www.iuniverse.com
1-800-Authors (1-800-288-4677)

ISBN: 978-1-5320-3054-3 (sc)
ISBN: 978-1-5320-3055-0 (e)

Print information available on the last page.

iUniverse rev. date: 09/20/2017

Carolyn Baker and Andrew Harvey have never been among those who stood on the sidelines peddling smoke: theirs was not a tincture of self-improvement, love and light. Neither have they been blissing out on peaceful mountain tops offering an order of transcendence with a side of spiritual bypass. Rather like biblical prophets, they have always stood in the middle of the flames, in the beauty and heartbreak of this world rooted deeply in the Heart of all matters. And this book is the culmination of their work-- the ultimate wake up call. -- **Vera de Chalambert, MTS, Author of "Kali Takes America," spiritual story teller and scholar of comparative religion**

Savage Grace examines the spiritual dimension of our existence as it informs and guides us in the disturbing and chaotic reality of our present times, yielding a sober, but far from pessimistic outlook. This is no mean feat, and Harvey and Baker have accomplished it admirably well. We know of no book like it.-- **Lydia and Nathan Schwartz-Salant**

"Savage Grace is that rare thing: a book that answers the needs of today by preparing us for tomorrow. It turns its steady gaze onto the unprecedented crises of our times and, with charged language equal to its subject matter, lays out specific, practicable means of readying ourselves for what is unfolding. Savage Grace is at once a surgical assessment, a handbook for action, and a compelling summons to realize our fullest humanity. Take this book into your heart and it will nourish what is best in you, even when you face the great unknown that is upon us all."
– Philip Shepherd, author of New Self New World: Recovering Our Senses in the Twenty-first Century, and Radical Wholeness: The Embodied Present and the Ordinary Grace of Being

"Truth is the gateway to the moment. It's also the portal to transformation. At this tenuous and horrifying moment in human history, nothing less will do. We either fiercely confront our challenges, or we slip noisily into the night. In Savage Grace, sacred activists Carolyn Baker and Andrew Harvey inspire us to wake the hell up before it's too late, while providing us with tools to navigate the crisis before us. This courageous book couldn't have arrived at a more perfect moment. Read it, and get to work! Now." **--Jeff Brown, author of 'An Uncommon Bond', and 'Soulshaping'**

In Savage Grace, Andrew Harvey and Carolyn Baker prove themselves once again to be among the most significant spiritual voices in our world.

--Marianne Williamson, author and spiritual teacher

"Cover Image: Kali, the dark goddess of destruction, death, rebirth, and transformation"

Dedication

With deepest love and gratitude to Joanna Macy,
grandmother of us all, a master teacher
of courage in dark times.

Contents

Foreword By Matthew Fox

This valuable book dares to speak a stark truth to both soul and society at this critical time in human and planetary history. There are those who say that maybe we have passed the point of no return for our species as we know it and the same for the planet as we have known it. This book offers some necessary medicine for surviving this time of apocalypse and undergoing the darkness that envelops us everywhere we turn--whether the seemingly dead-end politics of our time, or economics, or tired education and religion, and fear-driven media--all so numb and/or in denial in the presence of climate change, species extinction, sea level rise and more. No one seems safe from the cascade of bad news.

The great medieval mystic Meister Eckhart dared to say: "God is the denial of denial." To me this means that if denial is afoot, Divinity is absent; Truth is absent. This book cuts through denial. When denial dies, Spirit and Divinity are possible again--and hope. When John of the Cross, often accredited with the concept of the "dark night of the soul," escaped his prison and torture, he penned a poem we know as the "Dark Night," and in it he wrote that what saved him and gave him the courage to risk his life to escape was "a fire, a fire inside" that no one could extinguish. The fruits of studying this book must also be a rekindling of a fire, a fire inside us all if we are to be instruments of Mother Earth in her time of agony. It is time to forego the rhetoric about "loving our children and grandchildren" and commit to doing something about the diminished beauty and health and diversity of the planet that they face if we do not act wisely and generously and bravely today and start creating a new society and indeed, a new humanity--one that is in tune with the Earth and not objectifying her for our own greedy goals.

The eco-philosopher David Orr defines hope as "a verb with the sleeves rolled up," and I like this definition for it tells us that hope is conditional on our willingness to act. It is not enough to act superficially or in a reptilian brain mode of action/reaction, rather we must act now from a deep place of non-doing and non-action, that is from our being. That is why ours is a time not only for scientists and inventors but also mystics and contemplatives to join hands so that our action flows from being and from a deep place of return to the Source. Inner work as well as outer work is called for--and the courage to examine our intentions and our shadows and do that inner work of examining darkness even as we swim in it.

The "dark night of the soul" that the mystics talk about has descended on us all today. This book talks of the "dark night of the globe," and I have talked for years about the "dark night of our species." Some lessons from the mystics about the dark night are these:

1) It is a special and valuable place to be for we learn things here that we do not learn in the light: lessons of wisdom and often of compassion for example.

2) You will be tempted to flee, for the dark night is an uncomfortable place to find oneself. Flight may take many forms including addictions, denial, cover-up, passivity, couch-potato-itis, and a "let the others guys fix things" mentality.

3) Courage is required to stick around at such a time as the Sufi mystic Hafiz put it, "when God turns us upside down to shake all the nonsense out." A lot of nonsense needs shaking out today, much of it inherited from a modern consciousness that separated us from ourselves and the Earth and other species. This book speaks to those nonsense teachings that need to go and to what might supplant them.

4) Sometimes one tastes nothingness in times like this. Do not be afraid. Nothingness can turn on a dime to deep creativity. Dare to stick around and taste all that the darkness has to say to us. Silence too. Meister Eckhart once said: "I once had a dream— though a man, that I was pregnant--pregnant with nothingness. And out of this nothingness God was born."

5) Absence or near-absence of hope tempts us, yet despair is not a worthy option. St Thomas Aquinas says that while injustice is the worst of sins, despair is *the most dangerous.* Why? Because when a person or a community yields to despair, they do not love themselves and therefore do not care about others either. Feminist poet Adrienne Rich warns of a "fatalistic self-hatred" that accompanies patriarchy.

Such self-hatred can lead to despair. How then do we resist despair?

One way is to "look up to the mountains" as the Psalmist proposes. Look to the bigger picture. Let go of our anthropocentrism and narcissism (to use Pope Francis' words) to take in the more-than-human world again. Absorb the cosmos anew and with it the story and 13.8 billion year history that has brought us this far. Scott Russell Sanders in his powerful book, *Hunting for Hope: A Father's Journey,* puts it this way. "I still hanker for the original world, the one that *makes us* rather than the one we make. I hunger for contact with the shaping power that curves the comet's path and fills the owl's throat with song and fashions every flake of snow and carpets the hills with green. It is a prodigal, awful, magnificent power, forever casting new forms into existence then tearing them apart and starting over....That the universe exists at all, that it obeys laws, that those laws have brought forth galaxies and stars and planets and—on one planet, at least—life, and out of life, consciousness, and out of consciousness these words, this breath, is a chain of wonders. I dangle from that chain and hold on tight."

How tight are we hanging onto that chain of wonders that brought us into being? In this book Andrew Harvey and Carolyn Baker assist us in our dangling and holding on tight; and our wondering; and our healing and getting over ourselves; and our moving to a new moment in our evolution. Are we up to the task? Stay tuned.

Turning and turning in the widening gyre
The falcon cannot hear the falconer;
Things fall apart; the centre cannot hold;
Mere anarchy is loosed upon the world,
The blood-dimmed tide is loosed, and everywhere
The ceremony of innocence is drowned;
The best lack all conviction, while the worst
Are full of passionate intensity.
—"The Second Coming," William Butler Yeats

Shortly after the election of Donald Trump as President of the United States, we agreed to write this book because we were certain that people who have begun to awaken to the global crisis, those who had been awake to it for years, and even those who were not quite able to own it, let alone metabolize it, would need such a book. As we pondered numerous possibilities for a title, we chose *Savage Grace: Living Resiliently in The Dark Night of The Globe* because we believe that only unprecedented, *savage* grace can carry us through this era and that *resilience* is the absolute crux of how we must respond to the terrifying and daunting events unfolding in our time. The definition of resilience we prefer is: *The life-giving ability to shift from a reaction of denial or despair to learning, growing, and thriving in the midst of challenge.*

In order to grasp and live resilience, it is imperative that we become, as Jesus said, "wise as serpents and harmless as doves." Early on in this book, we share excerpts from an article we wrote together shortly after the election entitled, "The Serpent and the Dove: Wisdom for Navigating the Future." We are embracing living purposefully beyond illusion but also open to possibility even in the midst of what seems hopeless catastrophe.

What we did not quite understand initially was the extent to which we are now living in a post-truth, post-fact society—and the gruesome toll that is taking on all of us emotionally and spiritually. *The ultimate danger in living in a post-truth world is that eventually we develop the desire to be lied to.* Soon, we encountered an article by psychiatry professor, Ronald Pies, entitled "Alternative Facts: A Psychiatrist's Guide to Twisted Relationships to Truth"[1] in which the author states that the ultimate danger to us in a post-truth world is that eventually, we develop the desire to be lied to. Similarly, Adam Kirsch wrote in his *New York Times* article in January, 2017 "Lie to Me," that, "The problem with our 'post-truth' politics is that a large share of the population has moved beyond true and false. They thrill precisely to the falsehood of a statement, because it shows that the speaker has the power to reshape reality in line with their own fantasies of self-righteous beleaguerment. To call novelists liars is naïve, because it mistakes their intention; they never wanted to be believed in the first place. The same is true of demagogues."[2]

A crisis of the magnitude we are going through demands

the two most difficult things for human beings: Knowing how to negotiate extremely stressful ambiguity at all times while remaining humbly in a state of radical unknowing that is always open to the sometimes overwhelming shifts of an exploding disruption.

The great prophetic poet Milosz, poignantly attuned to the collapse of civilization in our time, wrote:

> When gold paint flakes from the arms of the sculptures
> When the letter falls out of the book of laws
> Then consciousness is naked as an eye.
>
> When the pages of books fall in fiery scraps,
> Onto smashed leaves and twisted metal,
> The tree of good and evil is stripped bare.[3]

As individuals who have stepped into the spiritual and cultural role of *elder*, our commitment is to speak to you with a consciousness as naked as an eye, without any desire to scare or flatter you. Because of that, we are presenting our material in as direct and precise a manner as we can.

However, as elders we know that reality always transcends any concepts that can be made of it, especially in a crisis as vast, volatile, and maddeningly complex and constantly evolving as this one. The concepts and maps we are going to share represent the distillation of our lifetimes of experience; they must be treated not as finally definitive but as pointers to what we believe is likely to happen and to the shifting responses that we believe now could be most effective and necessary as the crisis inevitably deepens.

Milosz wrote that in a time like ours, the tree of good

and evil is stripped bare. Those who know and suffer this are compelled to speak without any adornment or fear, since everything is at stake.

To some readers, our words may appear harsh, scolding, and impossibly demanding. We make no apology for this. Just as parents when faced with real problems or dangers to their children don't mince their words, we don't mince ours, out of urgent and surgical compassion. When a child is dancing toward the edge of a cliff unconsciously, a parent may scream and gesture wildly and if necessary, grab the child fiercely, but only to save the child's life. Great indigenous elders whom we revere have taught us that divine ferocity is an essential weapon in the armory of love.

In a time where denial reigns supreme and there is a corrupt emphasis in spiritual circles on a fake compassion, cheerfulness, and too-easy forgiveness coupled with a complete inability to face or respond to dire structural injustice, it is a very difficult task to tell the truth. People have been trained in habits they call spiritual but which really are designed to reinforce bypassing and dissociation.

To those who are just waking to the truly horrifying, even unbelievable severity of the crisis in which we find ourselves, we would like to say: Please listen to what we have to say, do the research that will validate what we say, and when you find yourself overcome by fear or the desire to turn away from what is now before us, don't judge yourself, because what you're feeling is entirely human. Instead, however shattered you are, and you inevitably will be, and however overwhelmed you find yourself by the facts, have the courage to do the deeper work of both creating a larger container from which to listen to stark news and advice and plunge into shadow work on yourself which will enable you to identify why you react in such a manner. This will enable you to become strong enough to resist the devouring madness and develop strategies with others of remedial and potentially inspired action.

We draw on all of the spiritual traditions and their wisdom because we realize that a new universal mysticism is being born that recognizes the contributions and wisdom of all the traditions. The necessity in our time demands that we listen to all of them for whatever guidance they can offer us in what is the defining evolutionary crisis of our entire human journey.

Some sections of this book will be challenging to read. We are not writing to persuade and convince those who have not yet understood the depth of our predicament. We are writing this book for those who know we are in a global dark night that could lead either to an unprecedented transformation or to extinction. The choice of "dark night of the globe" in our title is intentional because we believe that just as individuals experience a dark night of the soul, our species, indeed our planet, is experiencing a dark night.

Author and spiritual teacher Eckhart Tolle describes the dark night as "a collapse of a perceived meaning in life . . . an eruption into your life of a deep sense of meaninglessness. The inner state in some cases is very close to what is conventionally called depression. Nothing makes sense anymore, there's no purpose to anything. Sometimes it's triggered by some external event, some disaster perhaps, on an external level. The death of someone close to you could trigger it, especially premature death, for example if your child dies. Or you had built up your life, and given it meaning—and the meaning that you had given your life, your activities, your achievements, where you are going, what is considered important, and the meaning that you had given your life for some reason collapses."[4] In his writings, Eckhart states that he experienced his dark night almost continuously from early childhood until his thirtieth birthday, feeling suicidal daily. In his first spiritual book, *The Power of Now*, and subsequent books and teachings on being fully present, he describes his journey of awakening—a journey which is not unique to him but has been experienced by myriad individuals from numerous spiritual traditions.

Carl Jung also experienced a severe dark night of the soul at the age of thirty-eight, when he became emotionally overwhelmed by an invasion from the subconscious and saw visions and heard voices. Somehow, Jung had the clarity—and had built a container strong enough--to realize that what was happening was revelatory, and he brought himself back from disintegration, not by resisting his experience, but by having the fierce, sober courage to continue to dialog with it through journaling and a process he called *active imagination*. In a dark night experience, repressed contents of the unconscious surface, Jung concluded, to grab our attention, and through journaling, art, and dream work, one develops a dialog with these contents in order to integrate their extremely valuable messages into the psyche.

Without this difficult passage of integration, the psyche will either disintegrate into madness or maintain a precarious false stability which can easily be subverted and destroyed from within. The hundreds of millions of us now plunged into dark nights that are at once individual and collective need all the tools necessary and available to help us acquire what Jesus called "the wisdom of the serpent"—that wisdom that as Blake said, "is sold in the desolate market where none come to buy."[5] Only the marriage of this dark wisdom with the inner knowledge of our sacred identity with the divine which Jesus called "the innocence of the dove," can engender in us both the strength and the skillful suppleness of heart and mind that survival in our time demands.

What makes this marriage of serpent and dove in us both imperative and extremely difficult is that in addition to living in a post-truth era, we're also now clearly entrenched in a time of explosive, omnipresent, and potentially annihilating uncertainty that constantly shreds our minds and swirls darkly in our dreams. We do not know from one day to the next, sometimes from one moment to the next, what new manifestation of chaos will erupt: extreme weather, war, financial insecurity, mass shootings, revelations of extreme corruption in all of our institutions, and more. The global dark night we're in ensures that we are all in a state that mirrors in some ways advanced Post-Traumatic Stress Disorder. Studies of individuals living with PTSD suggest that the most distressing aspect of the trauma they suffered was the uncertainty of their predicament. According to Liji Thomas, M.D., "Uncertainty about the future makes us less capable of coping with negative events when they happen. It also disables us from taking effective and efficient steps to avoid them. This negative reaction is actually a maladaptation of the intrinsic ability of the human brain to predict the future, based on knowledge and past experience."[6] One of the characteristics of a dark night, as St. John of the Cross, Rumi, and others make devastatingly clear, is that nothing is predictable, and all systems of previously-achieved clarity collapse because they are now absurdly inappropriate.

What the great mystics of all the traditions who have survived this terrible passage tell us with one voice is that when we come to a dark night, we have only one resource: To remain in a state of *radical unknowing*. This will have two effects. It will crucify the false self's perpetual hunger for certainty, and it will flay us humbly open to the guidance that can only come if we are totally receptive to it with no preconceptions.

In *Nonsense: The Power of Not Knowing*, Jamie Holmes examines the concept of ambiguity and what often happens to us in the face of it. "The mind state caused by ambiguity," Holmes writes, "is uncertainty, and it's an emotional amplifier. It makes anxiety more agonizing, and pleasure more especially enjoyable."[7] Holmes explicitly states that he wrote the book in order to convince us that "in an increasingly complex, unpredictable world, what matters most isn't IQ, willpower, or confidence in what we know. *It's how we deal with what we don't understand*."[8] [Emphasis ours]

In reading *Nonsense*, we were riveted by the author's statement that "Nazism was partly fueled by the dangerous pairing of a hateful ideology with its adherents' inflated aversion to doubt."[9] As we attempt to navigate industrial civilization in collapse and a global trend toward authoritarian government, we feel in our own bodies and in our interactions with other individuals and communities the heightened anxiety produced by uncertainty. Even among many of our friends and acquaintances who are awake to the potential for near-term human extinction, we notice an implicit and almost-pathological demand for certainty. Many are obsessed with the year they believe humans will become extinct. Is it 2026, 2030, 2050, next year? As if we could know.

As elders we have been compelled to understand that authentic wisdom only arises out of a constant embrace of unknowing and uncertainty. This demands adamantine spiritual strength and a constant readiness to sacrifice even our most righteous certainties and every illusion about ourselves, human nature, and the purposes of the divine. In the Koran, Allah says, "For with God are the keys of the unseen; no one knows them but God. [10]

Our experience and our spiritual journeys have taught us that on myriad levels, age exacerbates uncertainty. In our youth we were far more "certain" about life and the future. We were "certain" in the 1960s that cultural revolution would lead to political revolution and the sudden death of capitalism. At times we were "certain" that a nuclear war was baked in the cake, and we would not live to see our fiftieth birthdays. We were certain in the early stages of the New Age that a massive spiritual movement would transform humanity. In fact, this movement failed to galvanize and transform. Many aspects of it were narcissistic and addicted to easy ways of transcendence. On the other hand, the sacred body was celebrated, and more radical forms of science were honored, alongside an increased tolerance for all paths. Yet given the scope of the crisis confronting us, the so-called New Age movement has failed spectacularly to inspire individuals to make radical enough changes both internally and in terms of external action.

This movement is now morphing among youth into

yoga, mindfulness, and a variety of neo-shamanic practices that rather than deepening awareness, are providing endless forms of spiritual bypassing. This is not to say that every person who engages in such practices is avoiding deepening, but frequently, the emphasis is on having ever- newer feel-good experiences rather than allowing oneself to be dragged by the anguish of the human condition into the depths of one's psyche.

All of our illusions have bitten the dust, and we are standing naked before a disintegrating history. Yet as we have increasingly claimed the role of elder, we have come to understand that real power lies not in certainty, but in *un*-certainty. As the poet, Jane Hirshfield, writes in her poem, "Against Certainty": "There is something out in the dark that wants to correct us. Each time I think 'this,' it answers 'that.'. . . Between certainty and the real, an ancient enmity."[11] What has increasingly amazed us, however, is that this 'ancient enmity' if you can endure it and make it conscious, becomes the dearest friend and shrewdest guide.

We must face that industrial civilization and its specific institutions totally dissociated from nature and indigenous wisdom are inherently traumatizing in ways we hardly recognize because we have lived with them for so long. We recommend further reading on the issue of trauma in industrial civilization as articulated by Judith Herman, Bessel van der Kolk, Peter Levine, and Gabor Maté. Any serious study of trauma in our culture quickly reveals that trauma is so pervasive and so normalized that we may easily miss that one of its central features is inevitably a dangerous obsession with certainty. How could it be otherwise in a culture that has provided us no sacred containers with which both to endure and to work with the potentially transformative nature of chaos? And yet, in our crisis of the global dark night, it is precisely this obsession with certainty that fuels catastrophe and makes almost impossible the creation of a new path that responds authentically to constantly shifting and explosive situations. Such a path cannot be wholly predictive, comforting, or clear-cut. It must embrace at all moments, paradox, ambiguity, and the prospect of extreme events and circumstances that compel wholly new alignments.

In this book we will speak about what we believe to be the potentially different stages of the unfolding crisis. In each stage, even the last, terminal one, we will suggest appropriate and helpful tactics. We know at this stage of our evolution that there dwells in us a force of awareness, truth, love, and commitment to service that will not be shaken by whatever happens. Our hope is that by the end of reading this book, you will not only be awoken to the severe truth of what's going on, but inspired to discover in yourself that Self that has never been born and will never die and that lives in a subtle and calm joy that no circumstances, even the most terrible, can destroy. The *Reconnection, Resistance, Resilience,* and *Regeneration* that we are going to celebrate in this book, arise from this Self and return to it. Our vision of resistance and activism does not depend on hopeful outcomes. It depends only on a resolute commitment to uphold, honor, and implement the dignity and consciousness of interrelationship that arise from the Self.

Let's get real and face together the likelihood that the human race now has two possibilities before it: An extreme crisis that leads to the survival of a bedraggled and traumatized remnant in a vastly degraded world, or the total annihilation of that world. We can never rule out, of course, the possibility of a sudden evolutionary leap in humanity or even miraculous divine intervention, but we would be narcissistic fools to count on them. We have come to the current situation because we have drunk a deadly cocktail of illusion. Our only hope now, rugged though it is, is in daring to live beyond the need for any kind of magical thinking—beyond, in fact certainty of any kind. We must take complete responsibility for the horror we have engendered and for the response we are now called to make to that horror, whatever happens. Such a response demands of us something far deeper than what conventional religions and visions of activism call for--nothing less than living and acting from the Self, both without illusion and totally committed to compassion and justice even, if necessary, in hopeless situations.

In this dark night of the globe, we have come to understand that four crucial strategies must be employed not only to survive the dark night, but to inhabit our bodies and our lives with passionate authenticity, honesty, vigilance, community, compassion, and service. These strategies are *Reconnection, Resistance, Resilience,* and *Regeneration.*

First of all, it is imperative that we understand how we arrived at this tragic juncture in the history of our species. We believe that our predicament is a result of profound *disconnection*—from our sacred inner wisdom, from all other living beings as a result of our delusional belief in separation, and from Earth and the reality that we are not only inherently connected with Earth, but that in fact, we *are* Earth. Thus, the first strategy must be a commitment to *Reconnection*.

Secondly, we must discern the nature of the myriad enemies of mind, body, and spirit with which we are being confronted in the current milieu and learn strategies of *Resistance* in order to take a stand in the Self for transparency and integrity in the face of massive assaults on our fundamental humanity.

Thirdly, we must cultivate extraordinary physical, emotional, and spiritual *Resilience* in order to navigate the plethora of dangers and uncertainties with which we are incessantly confronted. Resilience is an essential life skill that we have now to fine-tune both amid the turmoil of our daily existence as well as the monumental, explosive uncertainties we increasingly encounter in our communities and our world.

And finally, we must commit to living lives of *Regeneration* in all of the stages, even in what could be the terminal one. Even if humanity is destined to vanish, those of us who are awake to the responsibilities of love will work to ensure as far as possible that we leave the planet still just able to sustain and evolve new life. As with Sacred Activism[12] and the work of cultivating a vital spiritual path for our lives, what matters most is not the outcome of our efforts, but rather, our inmost intention.

Buddhist teacher and author, Margaret Wheatley, in her forthcoming book, *Who Do We Choose to Be?* states,

> This needs to be stated clearly at the outset: we can no longer solve the global problems of this time at large-scale levels: poverty, economics, climate change, violence, dehumanization.

Even though the solutions have been available for a very long time, they require conditions to implement them that are not available: political courage, collaboration across national boundaries, compassion that supersedes self-interest and greed. These are not only the failings of our specific time in history; they occur in all civilizations at the end of their life cycle.

This is a bitter pill for activists and all people with discerning, open hearts. We understand the complexity of global problems, we have thought systemically to define root causes, we have proposed meaningful solutions, but we are impotent to influence those in power who ignore our efforts.[13]

Wheatley states that she learned years ago that large-scale change is not possible because of the power of corporations, politicians, and leaders who treat people as units rather than as humans. The collapse of this system is now certain. What is also certain is that powerless though we now are to reverse the catastrophe of collapse, we are not powerless to create islands of sanity, rugged compassion, and dignified defiance amid a sea of chaos. How is this possible? By searching our souls in order to answer these questions:

- Who do I want to be in this devastating time?
- Who must we be together as we navigate the dark night of the globe?

If we are willing to focus with laser intensity on *Reconnection, Resistance, Resilience*, and *Regeneration* regardless of the eventual outcome of this crisis—regardless of whether or not it is even possible to survive it physically—in the words of Yeats, a "Second Coming" *is* possible. We can live passionate, purposeful, inspired lives even in terminal disaster. The only force stronger than hope is love, and love will be ours if we make it ours. And love, even in final circumstances will give us dignity, joy, and purpose. Thus a transformation of consciousness and relatedness can occur even more profoundly as that "rough beast—its hour come round at last, slouches toward Bethlehem to be born."

Andrew Harvey, Oak Park, Illinois

Carolyn Baker, Boulder, Colorado

Chapter 1

Kali Takes America: Reconnecting with the Destroyer/Creator

Kali, the Goddess of life and death, of creation and destruction, is the most revered Hindu goddess, beloved in India. But our country hasn't dealt with Kali at all because we don't like to think that death is part of life. . . . I mean, if we gave any thought to it at all, we'd know that death leads to new life. I think we have to learn to accept mystery, to accept that the Divine is mysterious and that if we think we know everything, we are grossly deceived.

—Marion Woodman, *Dancing in the Flames: The Dark Goddess in the Transformation of Consciousness*[14]

Shortly following the 2016 Presidential election in the United States, Harvard educated scholar of comparative religion, Vera de Chalambert, penned her extraordinary article "Kali Takes America: I'm With Her" at the *Rebelle Society* blog.[15] Almost instantly becoming viral, this audacious, astute piece pierced like a flaming sword the psyches of countless individuals who had already noticed the astonishing resemblance between Donald Trump and the destructive and chaotic forces he has unleashed and the Hindu goddess, Kali. Kali is destroyer and creator—killer of illusion and champion of liberation. Wearing around her neck a necklace made of skulls, she is infamous for death, sex, and violence on the one hand, yet she is also tender, passionate for justice, compassionate, and burning with an incomprehensible and blissful love. With Kali we are invited into an illusion-less confrontation and embrace of the paradoxes of life and creation. This confrontation and embrace demand nothing less than the death of our individual false selves and of the illusions and fantasies around which our social, economic, and political structures are flimsily constructed.

De Chalambert boldly declares Trump as mirroring the dark side of Kali and explains that whenever she appears, her terrifying presence is necessary because something demands to be urgently transformed. The author challenges our American addiction to "hope" and "optimism" and asserts that Kali is now here in our presence to strip us naked and have her ferocious way with us. "The mystics tell us that we need spiritual crisis," says De Chalambert. "That we must enter the Cloud of Unknowing, the deepest despair, the most profound darkness within, without hope, in order to grow spiritually. They call such a time of deep crisis, of great uncertainty, the Dark Night of the Soul. There, in our radical desperation, in our absolute abandonment, it is said, the Divine Doctor awaits. Holy Darkness was Her medicine all along."[16]

It is, in fact, the *darkness* that heals us, not our incessant, tenacious grasping for splinters of light and reassurance that everything is going to work out somehow. In fact, the blogger writes, "Darkness heals us without a spoonful of sugar; the wound is the gift, and this election is a good dose."[17]

In a time of catastrophic climate change, when it is impossible to have an intelligent discussion of the subject without the "E-word" (Extinction) entering the conversation; in a time when hundreds of species are going extinct daily; when economic inequality is more globally painful and pervasive than it has ever been; when endless war appears to be as normal as eating corn flakes; and when corporations, now considered "persons," dictate and dominate virtually every aspect of our lives and culture, Donald Trump, agent of Kali, is now Chief Executive of the most powerful nation on Earth. Or as Bill Moyers stated to Lawrence O'Donnell on MSNBC's "The Last Word," August 17, 2017, "During the campaign I believed that Trump was the foghorn for our collective, malevolent furies. Now I believe he *is* the malevolent fury."

We are writing some of these words the day following President Trump's withdrawal from the Paris Climate Accord. While this Accord is far from perfect and does not address ruthlessly enough the real issues, it is a first step. Symbolically, for the President to withdraw from it at this time sends a terrifying message that only money and corporate profit now matter at all. The survival of the human race is clearly not as important as next week's stock prices. What clearer image of our moral, spiritual, and political dereliction could we be given?

Kali Yuga Stages and Responses

None of this madness would have surprised the ancient

Hindu sages, who predicted the age in which we are now living. For them Kali Yuga represents the collapse of every kind of inner and outer coherence and personal and institutional forms of compassion, concern, and justice. Everything revered in previous ages and all forms of checks and balances within a culture are systematically and terrifyingly undermined and eventually destroyed, leading to the total annihilation of the culture and all of its living beings. In our era the most obvious indicator that Kali is indeed dancing ruthlessly is the collapse of industrial civilization that is now underway and the complete lack of moral responsibility or responding with justice and compassion.

The Hindu sages identified four stages of Kali's dance: Ominous, dangerous, severe, and lethal. We see the dance of Kali playing out in our time in the following way:

1) *The Ominous Stage* of Kali's dance began with the creation of a technological civilization rooted in a denial of the sacred feminine and in the belief that nature existed only to be exploited. The terrible injustices that characterized the early evolution of industrial civilization were exposed and excoriated by the great Romantic poets and the major philosophers of change such as Marx, Rousseau, and Walt Whitman, who saw quite clearly that the obsession with domination of nature and the worship of profit as the bottom line would lead to a soulless culture, massive and dangerous inequality, and a world of endless war for resources. They were not heeded, and so the next stage unfolded.

2) *The Dangerous Stage* then ensued with an orgy of frantic expansion, fueled by a fantasy of endless energy and resources undergirded by the delusion of infinite growth on a finite planet. This was denounced by ecologists and environmentalists and the majority of scientists who were aware of the horrific dangers such an orgy was engendering. However, very little was done to limit the destruction, and the culture in general continued in its addiction and denial, supported by a massive military industrial complex. Wars became exponentially more destructive with the creation of a nuclear bomb, and humanity grew accustomed to a semi-psychotic state of endless consumerism laced with perpetual anxiety. This lead inevitably to the frightening stage of the dance in which we find ourselves.

3) *The Severe Stage* has now obviously begun to unfold with very little significant environmental mitigation of the damage done to our ecosystems and the omnipotence of the 1% whose soulless pursuit of power and money at all costs dictates policy on every level. It is now only a matter of decades before the planet may be uninhabitable as a result of this dark marriage of addiction to power and total lack of any concern for compassion or justice or even survival. We must see this for what it is—a psychosis, unhealable by anything but catastrophe, and perhaps not even then; a nihilism that is, yes, demonic and that has rotted the human passion for transformation.

4) *The Lethal Stage*, a whole bevy of appalling facts makes clear, could soon be upon us. The lethal stage of Kali's dance will destroy human and animal life and a vast portion of the planet. In case this seems exaggerated, let us not forget that such destruction has occurred before with the extinction of the dinosaurs and the devastation of the Great Flood. More and more people are now realizing with the election of Donald Trump and the corruption, ignorance, blindness, and turpitude that attend and support his Presidency, that this is not only a possibility, it is a distinct probability.

Please do not read our description of these stages too quickly. Allow yourself to be exposed at visceral depths to what Kali is trying to teach us all whether we like it or not.

How Then to Move Forward?

There can be no way forward in a crisis as absolute and extreme as ours except through such terrifying knowledge. And this knowledge must lead to wise and skillful action if it is not itself to become corrupt and paralyzing.

When we wrote "The Serpent and the Dove: Wisdom for Navigating the Future" article,[18] we named three essential perspectives and actions that awake human beings must embrace going forward into what we know as a "Dark Night of the Globe," namely *Reconnection*, *Resistance*, and *Resilience*. We understood that the Age of Trump would be extremely challenging for all living beings on the planet in the face of his perspectives on economics, the environment, culture, foreign policy, and race--and the deranging they are marshaling, both in the corporate and political worlds.

Almost immediately after the Trump victory, many who voted against him and even those who did not vote at all began calling for "reconciliation" in order to ensure a peaceful transition of power. We believed that "reconciliation" could not be the most appropriate approach, since the values Trump had espoused so soundly alienated so many outside his campaign. Attempts at reconciliation are important, but we need to be very cautious because the word "reconciliation" is not stringent enough. The notion of reconciliation can easily continue the kind of comatose, fake inclusiveness that makes us vulnerable to deceit. The wise words of Jesus come to mind in which he counsels his followers to be wise as serpents and harmless as doves. In the current situation, we must beware of New Age soppiness and "let's love him no matter what" sentimentality. There is no authentic reconciliation without authentic discernment and without both parties opening their arms.

To reconcile too fast with a form of fascism that could usher in the last, lethal stage of Kali's dance is a dereliction of every kind of intelligence. It is reminiscent of a wife, repeatedly raped and battered, who clings to the belief that her husband can change if only she endures.

As a January, 2017, *New York Times* ad opposing the Inauguration of Trump states, "Trump is 'assembling a regime of grave danger' that is an 'immoral peril to the future of humanity and the earth itself.' Millions must rise up in a resistance with a deep determination such that we create a political crisis that prevents the Trump/Pence fascist regime from consolidating its hold on the governance of society."[19]

Post-election, CNN Republican commentator, Ana Navarro wrote that "It's hard to give Trump a chance when he staffs his White House with racists."[20] Post-election, comedian Dave Chappelle stated on *Saturday Night Live*[21] that he was willing to give Donald Trump a chance, but he asked that Trump give him a chance as well. Only in this kind of scenario, we believe, can authentic reconciliation have a prayer of succeeding. We cannot overemphasize the danger of a false rhetoric of reconciliation that does not realize both the depth of darkness of the forces now threatening our future and the enormous and ruthless power they possess and have shown they will use when they feel they must.

For this reason, we prefer using the word *Reconnection* as the first response we must make toward the rise of fascism, and this reconnection is not even primarily focused on the adversary. Without Reconnection, we simply will not be able to create a resistance movement. Reconnection fosters inner strength and a deeper connection with the truth of our own divine consciousness and the sacredness of creation. Reconnected, we are far more dynamically involved in creating community of every kind. *Reconciliation grounded in discernment can only occur when we are deeply reconnected with our inner wisdom of the Self, with Earth, and with our trusted and tried allies.* Unless we commit to doing the grueling and transforming work of Reconnection, no authentic reconciliation or necessary dialog with others of different perspectives can truly take place.

Our "Serpent and Dove" article did not provide us the

space we needed to elaborate on the deeper meaning of *Reconnection, Resistance,* and *Resilience,* which this book is intended to accomplish. Moreover, since writing the article, we believe a fourth 'R' should be added, namely, *Regeneration,* and this 'R' will be explored as it pertains to the other 'Rs' and the unfolding of the crisis.

We hasten to add that at the time of publication of this book, we do not see a robust, discerning resistance movement that has moved beyond feel-good activism. Although we celebrate all the acts of defiance that have revealed human decency and dignity, we nevertheless argue that a systemic illness lies at the core of industrial civilization, and that illness will bring about its collapse. For awake human beings, the purpose of the collapse, as with all suffering, is to transform our consciousness. Knowing that civilization will collapse, does not in any way preclude resistance and Sacred Activism. Not to resist and not to act, now ensures total destruction. Resistance and Sacred Activism are central to the transformation that is now taking place, but they both need to be enacted with unprecedented inner strength, discernment, and unwavering resolution. Resistance in our extreme circumstances must integrate activism with profound, soul-searching, soul-searing inner work in order to have any chance at all of being effective and transformative.

Possible Scenarios

We cannot afford at this moment any form of false hope or illusion. Kali humiliates such fantasies, and they will not serve us as we go forward. We envisage five possible scenarios:

1) A massive non-violent resistance movement rises imminently and prevents wholesale destruction.

2) A resistance movement that waxes then wanes as a result of being undermined by a post-truth, post-fact agenda in which the rampant corruption and the tendency toward violence that pervade the current administration paralyze the functioning of government and the willingness of citizens to resist.

3) Any resistance movement ruthlessly suppressed with the enactment of martial law, the silencing of the media, the incarceration and elimination of dissidents, and pervasive chaos throughout the culture signals the beginning of the fourth and final lethal stage of Kali's dance.

4) Modern civilization collapses, the planet is profoundly changed, much human and animal population is destroyed, some humans survive to seed the next churning of the human experiment in the post-apocalyptic world.

5) Horrifying suffering leading to the extinction of life on Earth.

These should not be perceived in any chronological order. Any of them could occur, and all might overlap.

In this book we want to explore how *Reconnection, Resistance, Resilience,* and *Regeneration* might manifest in all of these possible scenarios. Even if we realize that we are facing certain extinction, we are still responsible for the level of our consciousness in terms of how we treat others and how we attempt to mitigate the destruction that will be our only legacy.

In Carolyn's 2015 radio interview with Stephen Jenkinson, author of *Die Wise*, he spoke of the etymology of the Greek word *catastrophe,* noting that the prefix *cata*, implies moving downward and inward, and the suffix *strophe* relates to a kind of braiding or weaving activity. From Jenkinson's perspective, the deeper meaning of "catastrophe" is an entrance into the subtleties or mysteries of being a human being. That pathway has been established by people before us, and that road or braided rope is a way that we follow the descent into the mysteries of life.[22] Our work as awake human beings at this time then, is to be willing to descend into the dark night of the globe as well as the dark night of the individual soul and to do so in connection with trusted allies. Going downward and inward is the only way we can open to the mystery of the Self and be guided by it through whatever unfolds.

If you are reading these words, it is likely that you are on this road—a road traveled by many humans before you, but unique to you in this moment because you are facing challenges unlike theirs. Countless humans before us have faced catastrophe, and the fundamental concern of this book is not whether any of us will survive, but rather, how we face *cata-strophe* by following the call to go "downward" and "inward," and how we do so in deep connection with ourselves, each other, and Earth.

Reconnection

When we contemplate a future significantly shaped by a neo-fascist perspective, we will need much more than external dialog or benevolent intentions. In fact, when we speak of reconnection, interpersonal relationships are only one aspect of our concept of reconnection. Rather, we believe that reconnection of any kind must be grounded in reconnection with oneself, with the other, and with Earth. *Re*-connection assumes that a fundamental connection has been broken and cries out for restoration. The history of our species has been the history of humans attempting to connect and reconnect with self, other, and Earth. Our spiritual and religious practices throughout time have been designed for reconnection as in the etymology of the word *religion* or *religare,* which literally means "to bind back," that is to say, reconnect.

Reconnection is not without its price. You cannot reconnect with the truth of your divine Self, with other, and with Earth without being made aware of the excruciating intensity of all of the forces of dissociation and disconnection that now threaten life itself. Reconnection slaps you awake to your responsibility to live and act in a way that resists and transforms them.

As we find ourselves on a trajectory to human extinction as a result of climate catastrophe, what is essential is to reconnect at the deepest possible level with the Self, the divine within. This Self, as all the authentic mystical traditions reveal, is *not* the personal self. It is a universal, divine reality of which each one of us is a unique expression.

But, what does it mean to reconnect with Self? Is it yet another subtle form of the narcissism which has brought us to this tragic juncture in the human story? How do we connect with Self, yet remain connected with other and with Earth?

Let us begin by reevaluating the worth and truth of our emotions. William Blake was reported to have said that emotions are influxes of the divine, so perhaps our fundamental human emotions are pivotal in reconnecting with Self. Industrial civilization's disdain for emotion as "irrational" or "unscientific" has produced a modern human with a fragmented psyche and a heart entombed in a sarcophagus of nearly-numb insensitivity to anyone or anything or what we named in *Return to Joy* as a "flatline culture." What this disdain ensures is paralysis and denial in the face of the horror of the collapse of industrial civilization.

Four fundamental emotions which are certain to rise in a culture of neo-fascism are *fear, anger, grief,* and *despair* with variations of each. We often label these as "negative" emotions, but psychologist Miriam Greenspan in her wonderful book, *Healing through the Dark Emotions,* writes that, "Our distrust of the dark emotions has been heightened by recent mind-body research that concludes that negative emotions are bad for you, contributing to life-threatening illnesses from asthma to cancer, cardiovascular disease to immune system disorders. By and large, this research neglects to distinguish between emotions that are experienced mindfully—that is, fully experienced in the body in a direct and open way, as they occur—and those that are not mindfully experienced or have become "stuck" in the body."[23] In other words, so-called negative emotions are not inherently negative, but we often perceive them as such because we lack the tools to work with them consciously in order to mine the emotional and spiritual treasures that they hold for us.

In her 2011 book *Navigating the Coming Chaos: A Handbook for Inner Transition*, Carolyn noted that Greenspan speaks extensively of "emotional alchemy," drawing upon the ancient mystical practice of transforming baser metals into gold. By this she means that when we allow emotions to flow, which is not the same as merely "letting it all hang out," and when we allow grief, fear, despair, or other "negative" emotions in the body, we allow their wisdom to unfold. "Emotional flow," she says, "is a state in which one is connected to the energy of emotions yet able to witness it mindfully. We ride the wave of emotion on the surfboard of awareness. When we do this skillfully, emotional energy in a state of flow naturally moves toward healing, harmony, and transformation.[24]

Emotions have an extraordinary capacity to connect us with our own bodies because they issue *from* the body. Because we are so disconnected from our bodies, reconnection is most importantly reconnection with that body and the extraordinary wisdom of its changing, subtle reactions. Unless we learn how to revere, honor, and listen to our bodies, with deep compassion, reconnection with the Self is impossible. The reason is simple, the Self is not only transcendent but also immanent, and so, embodied. Likewise, when we share emotion with trusted allies, our connection with our emotions and the lives and bodies of our allies is immeasurably deepened, and often we enter the territory Rumi so beautifully described when he wrote, "Out beyond ideas of wrongdoing and rightdoing, there is a field. I'll meet you there."[25] Connections with our emotions and physical bodies enable us to reconnect viscerally with the creation. Moreover, the study of Ecopsychology increasingly reveals our emotional bond with Earth, and students of Ecopsychology and Permaculture often report the deep emotional connection they experience through engaging directly with soil, plants, and animals.

Beyond even our emotions and the rich and healing connection with Earth is the divine consciousness that all the mystical traditions know we have been originally blessed with. An entire plethora of techniques from simple meditation to the saying of the names of God in the heart are available. Everyone who fears for the future needs now to connect radically with the peace, joy, strength, persistence, and wisdom that our original birthright of divine consciousness makes possible and sustains. Claiming and experiencing our divine consciousness ends the illusion of separation from ourselves, each other, and Earth.

The illusion of separation is inherent in the paradigm of industrial civilization which flourished as a result of developing a "use" relationship with Earth. Whereas ancient and indigenous peoples experienced Earth as a living being with whom they cultivated an intimate relationship, modern, non-indigenous humans came to view the Earth as yet another resource that can be extracted from, commodified, and turned into profit. When we reconnect, we begin a long journey to subvert all the structures and ways of thinking and being of an obviously bankrupt civilization.

The Kali Yuga will become an era in which separation has never been more axiomatic. President Trump's cabinet is comprised of career "extractionists" whose fortunes have been acquired relentlessly through the commodification of

Earth and other living beings. Economic inequality, the exploitation of labor, and the deification of the corporation are becoming even more virulent than they have been in recent memory. Thus, human beings battered by the separation myth are likely to become more insatiably hungry for reconnection than at any previous time in our history. Therefore, everyone reading these words is now compelled to place reconnection with Self, others, and Earth at the center of their spiritual practice and functioning in the world. This is nothing less than an act of revolution with incalculable potential consequences for the future of our world. Any revolution that does not begin with this radically inclusive reconnection is doomed to failure.

If we do not commit to a conscious path of Reconnection, then all of our efforts toward Resistance and Resilience will not only fail, but lull us back into a mindset of business as usual and the delusion that "life goes on," *and* that our situation is something less than profoundly dire. And if we allow ourselves to be lulled to sleep by this now-obviously lethal fantasy, the greatest gift of our situation—it's clarion call for radical reconnection—will be unreceived, and with catastrophic consequences.

Since the 1970s, industrial civilization has commodified and extracted beyond anything humans on this planet have been able to achieve in their history. As a result, we created unprecedented emissions of CO_2 and the most massive extractions on Earth. We have all ridden this wave of fossil fuel use, brought all of our ingenuity to it, and have maximized extraction beyond anything the human species has ever done. The only metric we have used is profit, and the bottom line has been our Holy Grail. However, this has created a colossal blind spot in which we have initiated a trajectory of annihilating all life on Earth, and we are on the way to total systems collapse and near-term human extinction. All of this because we have disconnected from ourselves, from others, and from Earth. Our blind spot is our undoing because, since nature abhors a vacuum, when there is a blind spot, the human shadow will find its way into that spot.

In *No Is Not Enough: Resisting Trump's Shock Politics and Winning the World We Need,* Naomi Klein emphasizes that "...there is an important way in which Trump is not shocking. He is the entirely predictable, indeed clichéd outcome of ubiquitous ideas and trends that should have been stopped long ago. Which is why, even if this nightmarish presidency were to end tomorrow, the political conditions that produced it, and which are producing replicas around the world, will remain to be confronted. With US Vice-President Mike Pence or House Speaker Paul Ryan waiting in the wings, and a Democratic Party establishment also enmeshed with the billionaire class, the world we need won't be won by just replacing the current occupant of the Oval Office."[26]

What is more, says Klein, "...the ground we were on before Trump was elected is the ground that produced Trump. Ground many of us understood to constitute a social and ecological emergency, even without this latest round of setbacks."[27]

Another socio-political factor that laid the groundwork for a Trump victory is the abject despair experienced by masses of Americans who have lost more than jobs, houses, and dreams in recent decades. They have, in fact, lost faith in the American Dream itself, and if they have not succumbed to the opioid epidemic ravaging parts of the American Rust Belt or Appalachia, they may have been seen waving banners or taking cell phone shots of Trump at one of his numerous campaign rallies throughout Middle America.

Naomi Klein argues that the degradation of the idea of the public sphere or what is also known as "the commons"—a degradation which has been unfolding over decades, particularly since Ronald Reagan proclaimed that "government is not the solution; it is the problem,"[28] ultimately led to economic decline and made Trump's appeal possible. Fueled by the outrageous seductions of individualism and materialism in the 1980s and 90s and subsequent deregulation of corporations, alongside appalling sums of money flowing into politics, a "self-described billionaire sitting on a golden throne" was able to "pass himself off as a savior of the working class," says Klein. "A pitch as patently irrational as 'Trust me *because* I cheated the system' could only have been sold to a significant portion of the American public because what passed for 'business as usual' in Washington well before Trump, looked a whole lot like corruption to everyone else."[29]

Reconnecting with the Shadow

To begin with a simple definition, the shadow is any part of us that doesn't match with our ego image of ourselves and that we unconsciously send away and say, "That's not me." For example, I'm not a dishonest person; I'm not insensitive; I'm not greedy; I don't consider myself and my needs to be superior to the needs of other living beings.

While helpful, such a simple definition does not begin to explore the mystery and depth of the shadow, both in the ways it appears in reality in our lives and in the vast and very troubling questions such an exploration raises about the nature of the divine and reality itself. After all, one of Jung's greatest and most controversial achievements was to raise the question of whether the divine itself has a ferociously dark side.

Jung wrote in *Psychology and Alchemy*, "The shadow personifies everything that the subject refuses to acknowledge about himself and yet is always thrusting itself upon him directly or indirectly." He adds, "The shadow does not consist of small weaknesses and blemishes, but of a truly demonic dynamic."[30] Jung did not use the word *demonic* for effect. He used the word *demonic* because it is through our shadow that the destructive forces that are part of the alchemically creative nature of the One wreak their havoc, violence, suffering, and destruction.

Each of us has a personal shadow, briefly defined above, as well as a collective shadow. This is true for nations, cultures, and communities that essentially agree unconsciously that whatever bad behavior they name, that nation or culture or community says, "That's not us."

When we deny the individual or collective shadow, we ensure that we project it onto others in ways that can become deadly and extremely violent. This is why Jung said the shadow has nothing less than a demonic dynamic, and the history of the world is the story of this demonic dynamic.

Shortly after the election of Donald Trump, we often heard the question, "How could this have happened?" Only from a profound lack of awareness regarding the shadow could such a question have originated. Months later, Lebanese-American writer Rabih Alameddine in his *New Yorker* article, "Our Part in the Darkness," wrote:

> We are not better than this. We are this. The man was elected President. *Ipso facto,* America is this, we are this. I say this not to suggest that we must be blamed, or that someone who did not vote for Donald Trump is just as culpable as one who did. What I keep trying to point out, to friends, to anyone who will listen, is that too few of us are willing to acknowledge responsibility—not necessarily to accept blame, but to stand up and say, "This thing of darkness, I acknowledge mine."[31]

What does it actually mean to acknowledge that "this thing of darkness, I acknowledge mine"? It means accepting that we live, participate in, and collude with a culture that worships only money and success; that adores power, and denigrates love, compassion, and justice; and that each one of us has been contaminated by this culture's complete lack of conscience, responsibility, and obscenely superficial values. It means that we have learned to lie for our own advantage, to scheme to ensure our domination of others and build our security and that we all are paying the spiritual price in paralysis, cynicism, and despair. In fact, what this ferocious shadow work reveals is that we are as responsible for this situation as those whom we can conveniently characterize as its Darth Vaders and Genghis Khans.

This is a terrible recognition that all of us would love to

avoid; however, it leads to the kind of self-knowledge we all now need to negotiate with the other inmates of a worldwide madhouse. If we do not recognize our own insanity and the ways in which it deforms and informs our increasingly chaotic actions, how will we ever have compassion for others driven by the same dark whirlwind, and how will we ever evolve the skillful means to attempt to deal with them beyond the corrupt safeties of judgment and condemnation?

Reconnection Alongside Resistance and Resilience

As we have been emphasizing, the only legitimate ground on which to stand as we resist a neo-fascist agenda is the ground of intimate connection with the Self, each other, and Earth. Dean Walker, author of *The Impossible Conversation: Choosing Reconnection and Resilience at the End of Business as Usual,* argues that unwillingness to discuss the severity of catastrophic climate change and a number of other topics dealing with our planetary predicament results not only from the fear of facing the issues directly, but from our profound disconnection from Self, other, and Earth. Taken together, these make the issues strangely surreal and out of reach, and any discussions we have about them are ventures into the absurd.

Perhaps nothing is more blatantly indicative of our disconnection from Self, other, and Earth, than our current climate catastrophe. In *The Impossible Conversation*, Dean Walker devotes a relatively small but essential section of the book to what he calls the Sober Data. Here are seven factors in a long litany of unarguable and shattering facts:

1) The Earth is in the midst of a mass extinction of life. Scientists estimate that 150–200 species of plant, insect, bird and mammal become extinct every 24 hours. This is nearly 1,000 times the 'natural' or 'background' rate and, say many biologists, is greater than anything the world has experienced since the vanishing of the dinosaurs nearly 65 million years ago.

2) The World Wildlife Fund and Zoological Society of London's bi-annual report, Living Planet, assesses how the natural world is reacting to the stresses implied by an ever growing human population. Their study of over 3,700 vertebrate species shows that global wildlife populations have decreased by nearly 60% since the 70s.

3) The loss of fresh water animals is far greater, closer to 80%.

4) The amount of global coral reefs dead due to acidification and other human caused impact = 50%. If the current rate of warming and destruction continues, 90% of coral reefs will be threatened by 2030, and all of Earth's coral reefs could be dead by 2050. Within those same projections, the Great Barrier Reef would die by 2030.

5) It is both fascinating and devastating that scientists use the metric of 'atomic-bombs-worth of warming' on Earth and particularly within the Earth's oceans. Scientists have long known that more than 90 percent of the heat energy from man-made global

warming goes into the world's oceans instead of the ground.

6) The world's oceans will be empty of fish by 2048 due to overfishing, pollution, habitat loss and climate change. This projection is from an international research team that studied: data from 32 related experiments on marine environments, analysis of 1,000 year history of 12 coastal regions, fishery data from 64 large marine ecosystems and the recovery of 48 protected ocean areas. 'This isn't predicted to happen. This is happening now,' writes Nicola Beaumont, PhD, Plymouth Marine Laboratory, UK.

7) The worst thing that can happen is not energy depletion, economic collapse, limited nuclear war, or conquest by a totalitarian government. As terrible as these catastrophes would be for us, they can be repaired within a few generations. The one process ongoing that will take millions of years to correct is the loss of genetic and species diversity by the destruction of natural habitats. This is the folly that our descendants are least likely to forgive us.[32]

Contemplating the Sober Data, chosen almost at random, forces us to ask, "How did we arrive at our current predicament?" We concur with Dean Walker that our massive and largely unconscious disconnection from Self, other, and Earth has brought us to the ghastly, unprecedented predicament in which we are irreversibly ensnared.

In 2016, Carolyn and Dean began facilitating twice-monthly online calls with individuals who are eager to engage with each other in the "impossible conversation" in a heartfelt manner. Named Safe Circle calls, these online encounters have become a prototype for the kind of reconnection required for resistance as well as living resiliently.

If we do not reconnect with each other by sharing our heartbreak, we will not be able to resist or live resiliently. What is more, the Safe Circle call model creates a consistent container for discussing and mobilizing strategies of resistance and employing the fundamental tools of resilience.

To attempt to resist while lacking an understanding of reconnection and consciously utilizing reconnection practices, increases one's vulnerability and guarantees exhaustion resulting from struggling in isolation. Our resistance must be informed by robust connection with Self, other, and Earth. Moreover, to attempt to live resiliently without reconnection is to miss the essence of resilience. As stated above, resilience is *"the power or ability to return to the original form, position, etc., after being bent, compressed, or stretched; elasticity."*

Reconnection practices and resistance alongside trusted allies strengthen our resilience.

Suggested Practices

**Dedicate one day to taking a personal inventory of ways in which you are disconnected from yourself, others, and Earth. Notice the ways in which you are disconnected from your body. How are you disconnected from your emotions? How are you disconnected from other living beings? How are you disconnected from Earth?

**Are you engaged in any practice that connects you with your body such as yoga, Chi Gong, Tai Chi? If not, consider engaging in one of these practices. While regular fitness exercises are useful, they often do not connect us with the body's deeper energy and wisdom.

**With a trusted ally in your life, share one emotion you are feeling as you reflect on our global predicament. As much as possible, speak from your heart and not your head. Also invite your ally to share with you and listen carefully and attentively to them as they speak.

**Spend at least 15–20 minutes (or more) in the solitude of nature. If you are not used to doing this, it may be challenging at first. Simply sit or stand in nature and observe what is around you. Notice the smells, sounds, and textures of the elements of nature as well as colors, light, and shadow. Touch the trees, leaves, water, and soil. Return to this same place in nature within a few days. This time, take a notebook with you and write down what you notice. Be specific. As soon as possible, perhaps the next day, return to your solitude spot with your notebook and write down anything different that you notice. Continue this practice as often as possible, writing down what looks or feels different from time to time.

**Say the Name of the divine by whatever name you know it repeatedly in the depths of your heart. Over time, you will be initiated by grace into the truth of your non-dual relationship with the divine and into the depths of the strength, peace, truth, and wisdom of your deathless, divine Self.

Chapter 2

Resisting the Modern Face of Fascism in the Age of Trump

To recover our mental balance we must respond to Trump the way victims of trauma respond to abuse. We must build communities where we can find understanding and solidarity. We must allow ourselves to mourn. We must name the psychosis that afflicts us. We must carry out acts of civil disobedience and steadfast defiance to re-empower others and ourselves. We must fend off the madness and engage in dialogues based on truth, literacy, empathy and reality. We must invest more time in activities such as finding solace in nature, or focusing on music, theater, literature, art and even worship—activities that hold the capacity for renewal and transcendence. This is the only way we will remain psychologically whole. Building an outer shell or attempting to hide will exacerbate our psychological distress and depression. We may not win, but we will have, if we create small, like-minded cells of defiance, the capacity not to go insane.
"American Psychosis," article by Chris Hedges[33]

Resistance is first of all a matter of principle and a way to live,

to make yourself one small republic of unconquered spirit.
—Rebecca Solnit, *Hope in the Dark*[34]

In 2017 we are witnessing the rise of neo-fascist movements around the world. Europe has moved steadily to the right politically as austerity has pummeled the middle and working classes economically and as masses of Syrian refugees have sought sanctuary and asylum from the war-torn horrors of the Middle East. Currently, the political drift toward the right does not yet technically fit the definition of fascism, but rather, an alarming trend toward populism with a conservative and authoritarian, rather than liberal, trajectory.

In her November, 2016 *Guardian* article, "How the right invented a phantom enemy,"[35] Moira Weigel addresses the US election victory of Donald Trump as emblematic of the global wave of populism. As disbelieving pundits who proclaimed that he could never win the presidency stood in jaw-dropping disbelief on election night, the maverick candidate deftly sailed past the polls and the pundits toward victory in the US Electoral College by way of his use of an anti-politically correct agenda. Nearly every Trump stump speech and a host of his Tweet torrents contained remarks such as, "I refuse to be politically correct," or "I don't frankly have time for political correctness."

But Trump has not been alone in his rebellion against political correctness as Weigel notes. "Britain's rightwing tabloids issue frequent denunciations of 'political correctness gone mad' and rail against the smug hypocrisy of the 'metropolitan elite'. In Germany, conservative journalists and politicians are making similar complaints: after the assaults on women in Cologne last New Year's Eve, for instance, the chief of police Rainer Wendt said that leftists pressuring officers to be *politisch korrekt* (politically correct) had prevented them from doing their jobs. In France, Marine Le Pen of the Front National has condemned more traditional conservatives as 'paralysed by their fear of confronting political correctness'."[36] Fortunately, Marine Le Pen was defeated in her run for President of France, May 7, 2017.

The term *political correctness* is what ancient Greek rhetoricians would have called an "exonym," a term for another group, which signals that the speaker does not belong to it. Nobody ever describes themselves as "politically correct." The phrase is only ever used as an accusation.

Weigel argues, and we agree, that political correctness is a ruse created by the right, which it never fully defines, but bandies about in order to appear apolitical. In a world in which middle and working-class voters feel economically and culturally battered by the policies of neoliberal globalists, the prospect of an 'apolitical' leader is highly enticing. What is more, "PC was a useful invention for the Republican right because it helped the movement to drive a wedge between working-class people and the Democrats who claimed to speak for them. 'Political correctness' became a term used to drum into the public imagination the idea that there was a deep divide between the 'ordinary people' and the 'liberal elite', who sought to control the speech and thoughts of regular folk. Opposition to political correctness also became a way to rebrand racism in ways that were politically acceptable in the post-civil-rights era."[37]

On the other hand, many people still view Trump as

somewhat of a buffoon who is recklessly attempting to turn the entire political landscape on its head, and some even opine that this may, in fact, be healthy for the republic. However, if Trump's antics were merely political gymnastics intended to shake up the neoliberal world order, the entire spectacle might serve a higher purpose. However, as Weigel writes, "The opponents of political correctness always said they were crusaders against authoritarianism. In fact, anti-PC has paved the way for the populist authoritarianism now spreading everywhere. Trump is anti-political correctness gone mad."[38]

What is more, when we view Trump's authoritarian trajectory in the context of a global political drift toward the right, when we more carefully examine the individuals with whom he has surrounded himself as advisors and cabinet heads, and when we consider his own personal psychological profile, so extensively written about during his electoral campaign, we are astounded with the potential that is emerging for all-encompassing fascism in the United States.

But what exactly is fascism, and does it always appear in the form of Hitler's Germany in the 1930s or Mussolini's Italy or Franco's Spain? One of the most comprehensive books on modern fascism is *The Anatomy of Fascism* by Robert Paxton. He writes:

> Fascism may be defined as a form of political behavior marked by obsessive preoccupation with community decline, humiliation, or victimhood by compensatory cults of unity, energy, and purity, in which a mass-based party of committed nationalist militants, working in uneasy but effective collaboration

with traditional elites, abandons democratic liberties and pursues with redemptive violence and without ethical or legal restraints, goals of internal cleansing and external expansion.[39]

Paxton also describes the energy of fascist movements as the "mobilizing of passions."

Reflecting on the campaign of Donald Trump, one certainly sees the obsessive preoccupation with community decline as he incessantly described the policies of former administrations as "a disaster" and America's infrastructure as "a disaster" and American inner city life as "a disaster." We clearly hear victimhood in the notion that Trump was not being treated fairly by the media and that traditional elites were persecuting him. Exuding machismo with every bellicose roar, from "lock her up" to "we're going to build a wall," violence permeated Trump rallies where protestors were rounded up and ejected as the candidate bellowed, "Get 'em otta here." Threats of creating a registry for Muslims and even banning their entry into the United States, as well as the notion of building a wall between Mexico and the United States in order to curtail immigration resound with the fantasy of internal cleansing.

The Primary Features of Fascism

In his Farewell Address to The Nation in 1961, President Dwight Eisenhower warned:

In the councils of government, we must guard against the acquisition of unwarranted influence, whether sought or unsought, by the military-industrial complex. The potential for the disastrous rise of misplaced power exists and will persist.

We must never let the weight of this combination endanger our liberties or democratic processes. We should take nothing for granted. Only an alert and knowledgeable citizenry can compel the proper meshing of the huge industrial and military machinery of defense with our peaceful methods and goals, so that security and liberty may prosper together. [40]

This devastating prophecy has come true and creates the compost for the terrible black rose of fascism. In 1886, corporations were declared persons in a tragic United States Supreme Court decision. An even more tragically destructive decision was made by the Supreme Court in 2015 with regard to Citizens United which consolidated this notion but gave corporations as persons the legally sanctioned capacity to dominate and largely determine the political process. This indeed produced, as Greg Palast notes, "the best democracy money can buy."[41]

In 1995, Umberto Eco, the late Italian intellectual giant and novelist most famous for *The Name of the Rose*, wrote a guide describing the primary features of fascism. As a child, Eco was a loyalist of Mussolini, an experience that made him quick to detect the markers of fascism later in life, when he became a revered public intellectual and political voice. Eco made the essential point, which we need to remember, that *fascism looks different in each incarnation, morphing with time and leadership, as "it would be difficult for [it] to reappear in the same form in different historical circumstances."* It is a movement without "quintessence." Instead, it's a sort of "fuzzy totalitarianism, a collage of different philosophical and political ideas, a beehive of contradictions."[42]

In her 2016 Alternet article, "Trump Is an Eerily Perfect Match with a Famous 14-Point Guide to Identify Fascist Leaders," Kali Holloway (yes, her first name is Kali) summarizes the ways in which Donald Trump conforms to Eco's 14-point guide:

1) **The Cult of Tradition:** Let's make America great again. Holloway asks, "Remind me when America was great, again? Was it during the eras of native people genocide, slavery, black lynchings as white entertainment, Japanese-American internment, or Jim Crow?"

2) **Rejection of Modernism:** Trump denies climate change and supports fracking and opposes environmental regulations that protect the land and people from its devastations. He favors cuts to NASA and critical bio-medical research. Likewise, Mike Pence is a fervent denier of science and a religious zealot. He has taken a wait-and-see attitude on evolution and advocated for teaching intelligent design and creationism in schools. In a 2000 op-ed he wrote that "smoking doesn't kill," and penned a 2009 op-ed against embryonic stem cell use. Pence has written that global warming is a "myth," that the earth is cooling, and that there is "growing skepticism" among scientists about climate change—all the literal opposite of the

truth. He also opted to pray instead of immediately changing a law that would have stunted the spread of HIV, resulting in the worst HIV outbreak in Indiana history.

3) **The Cult of Action for Action's Sake:** For example, as Holloway notes "Anti-intellectualism and pride in idiocy—and disdain for complexity— are trademarks of today's Republican ideology. In this light, educated elites are the enemies of salt of the earth, hard-working (white) Americans. Their hatred of Obama was paired with disdain for what they view as his 'effete snob[bery]' and proclivity for lattes and arugula." In addition, "He [Trump] told the *Washington Post* he has 'never' read much because he makes decisions based on 'very little knowledge . . . because I have a lot of common sense.' Since winning the election, Trump has waived the daily intelligence briefings that far better-prepared and knowledgeable predecessors made time for, despite his being the first president with no experience in government or the military."

4) Opposition to Analytical Criticism; Disagreement Is Treason: According to Holloway, "Trump attempts to quell the slightest criticism or dissent with vitriol and calls for violence. On the campaign trail, Trump encouraged his base's mob mentality, promising to 'pay for the legal fees' if they would 'knock the crap' out of protesters. He gushed about 'the old days' when protesters would be 'carried out on a stretcher.' When the media finally began taking a critical tone after giving him

billions in criticism-free press, Trump declared his real opponent was the 'crooked press.' He pettily stripped reporters of press credentials when they wrote something he didn't like, referred to individual reporters as 'scum,' 'slime,' 'dishonest' and 'disgusting,' and claimed he would 'open up' libel laws so he could sue over unfavorable—though not erroneous—coverage. In the latter stages of the campaign, Trump supporters took to berating the media with shouts of 'lügenpresse,' a German phrase popular with Nazis that translates as 'lying press.' Some Trump supporters also sported T-shirts suggesting journalists should be lynched."

5) **Exploiting and Exacerbating the Natural Fear of Difference**: "The first appeal of a fascist or prematurely fascist movement is an appeal against the intruders," Eco notes. "Thus Ur-Fascism is racist by definition." Explaining how this plays out in Trump's world, Holloway writes that "Before he officially threw his hat into the ring, Trump courted bigots and racists furious about Obama's wins by pushing the birther lie and attempting to delegitimize the first black president. The only coherent policy proposals Trump made during his run were those that appealed to white racial resentments, promising to end Muslim immigration, build a wall along the southern border to keep Mexicans out and retweeting white nationalists' made-up statistics about black criminality."

6) **Appeal to Frustrated Middle Classes**: "Eco writes that fascism reaches out to 'a class suffering

from an economic crisis or feelings of political humiliation, and frightened by the pressure of lower social groups'." Clearly, Holloway argues, "Trump made overt appeals to whites who believe the American Dream is not so much slipping from their grasp as being snatched away by undeserving immigrants and other perceived outsiders. Trump made impossible promises to return manufacturing jobs and restore class and social mobility to a group of people nervous about falling down rungs on the ladder."

7) **Obsession with a Plot, Possibly an International One:** Holloway writes that, "Trump obviously appealed to racial and religious nationalist sentiments among a majority of white Americans by scapegoating Mexican and Muslim immigrants on issues of crime, job losses and terrorism. He pushed the idea that he would 'put America first,' suggesting that Hillary Clinton would favor other nations over the U.S." President Lyndon Johnson reportedly said, "If you can convince the lowest white man he's better than the best colored man, he won't notice you're picking his pocket." Unquestionably, Trump used this tactic with his supporters to scapegoat people of color, foreigners, and President Obama as responsible for the suffering of white working and middle-class Americans.

8) **Followers Must Feel Humiliated by the Ostentatious Wealth and Force of Their Enemies:** Holloway aptly summarizes this: "Trump conjured up a vision of America in a downward spiral, a

nation fallen from its lofty position in the world to one deserving of shame and ridicule. He spent much of the campaign telling Americans they weren't just losing, but had become the butt of an embarrassing worldwide joke." Throughout the campaign, Trump hammered home the notion that our enemies are laughing at us and that we have been made the laughing stock of the world.

9) **Pacifism Is Trafficking with the Enemy. It's Bad Because Life Is Permanent Warfare:** Holloway points out that "Trump has made expansion of the U.S. military a primary aim, putting the country in a perpetually defensive stance. In the past, he has reportedly demanded to know why the U.S. shouldn't use its nuclear weapons. In the weeks following the election, he filled his cabinet with war hawks. On the campaign trail, Trump said his generals would have 30 days following his election to put together 'a plan for soundly and quickly defeating ISIS.' The Center for Strategic and International Studies predicts that military spending under Trump may increase by $900 billion over the next decade." Trump also stated, "I'm gonna build a military that's gonna be much stronger than it is right now. It's gonna be so strong, nobody's gonna mess with us."

10) **Popular Elitism:** Astutely, Holloway grasps one of the principal lynchpins of the Trump world view. "Trump repeatedly hails himself as the best. He has the best words, the best ideas, the best campaign, the best gold-plated penthouse, the best of all the best of

the best things. Trump and his nationalist followers believe that America is the greatest country that has ever existed. That somehow makes Americans the best people on Earth, by dint of birth. In keeping with a long-standing right-wing lie about patriotism and love of country, conservatives are the best Americans, and Trump supporters are the best of all." Additionally, Eco wrote that "aristocratic and militaristic elitism cruelly implies contempt for the weak." As Holloway reminds us, "Trump biographer Michael D'Antonio has written that Trump's father instilled in his son that 'most people are weaklings,' and thus don't deserve respect. Trump, who has earned a reputation as a lifelong bully in both his public and private lives, has consistently bemoaned America's weakness, resulting from the reign of weak cultural elites."

11) **Everybody Is Educated to Become a Hero:** "Trump's base believes itself to be the last of a dying (white) breed of American heroes," says Holloway, "enduring multiculturalism and political correctness to speak truth to the powerful elites and invading hordes of outsiders who have marginalized and oppressed them, or taken what's rightfully theirs. Eco writes that "this cult of heroism is strictly linked with the cult of death . . . the Ur-Fascist hero craves heroic death, advertised as the best reward for a heroic life. The Ur-Fascist hero is impatient to die. In his impatience, he more frequently sends other people to death."

12) **Transfer of Will to Power in Sexual Matters:**
We've heard it all so many times, but Holloway
reminds us again that, "We are well acquainted
with Trump's machismo, which like all machismo,
is inseparable from his loudly broadcast misogyny.
This is a man who defended the size of his penis
in the middle of a nationally televised political
debate. For 30 years, including the 18 months of his
campaign, Trump has consistently reduced women
to their looks or what he deems the desirability
of their bodies, including when talking about his
own daughter, whom he constantly reminds us he
would be dating if not for incest laws. Trump has
been particularly vicious to women in the media,
tweeting insults their way, suggesting they're having
their periods when they ask questions he doesn't
like, and verbally attacking them at rallies and
inviting his supporters to follow suit. There's also
that notorious leaked 2005 recording of Trump
discussing grabbing women by the genitalia, which
was followed by a stream of women accusing him
of sexual assault."

13) **Selective Populism:** "Since no large quantity of
human beings can have a common will," Eco writes,
"the Leader pretends to be their interpreter. . . ."
Holloway elaborates, "There is in our future a TV or
internet populism, in which the emotional response
of a selected group of citizens can be presented and
accepted as the Voice of the People. Eco's two-
decade-old prediction is uncanny. Trump, a fixture
on social media and reality television, has mastered

a kind of TV and internet populism that makes his voice one with the angry masses of his base. At the Republican National Convention, after a rant about the terrible, dystopian shape of the country, he designated himself the nation's sole savior. 'I am your voice,' Trump said. 'No one knows the system better than me. Which is why I alone can fix it'." Holloway asks, "Is there any more vivid example of Eco's example than Trump's repeated contention that the election was rigged? Trump painted himself as the savior of a people who could no longer rely on rich, powerful politicians. Save for him, of course."

14) **The Use of Newspeak:** "All the Nazi or Fascist schoolbooks made use of an impoverished vocabulary, and an elementary syntax, in order to limit the instruments for complex and critical reasoning," Eco writes. "But we must be ready to identify other kinds of Newspeak, even if they take the apparently innocent form of a popular talk show." Summarizing, Holloway notes, "Trump also kept his sentences short and his words to as few syllables as possible. He repeated words he wanted to drive home, and punctuated his speech with phrases meant to have maximum effect. In lots of cases, a single quote contained multiple contradictory statements. The takeaway from a Trump speech was whatever the listener wanted to hear, which turned out to be a winning strategy."

We encourage our readers to read and study Holloway's coverage of Umberto Eco's article.[43]

While we could devote a significant amount of ink in this

book to examining in depth the politics and backgrounds of Trump's advisors and appointees to further demonstrate the potential for a sweeping wave of neo-fascism, we do not believe this is necessary in order to validate our assertion that the Western world is moving quite predictably and quite swiftly in that direction.

Furthermore, as Carolyn has been writing and researching for more than a decade, the collapse of industrial civilization is a foregone conclusion and is well underway. As in the case of a patient with a terminal illness, a nation spiraling downward may grasp at straws and numerous healing elixirs in order to resuscitate itself. Certainly, the snake oil of fascism appeals to the narcissistic, authoritarian reality TV star and the masses who hang on his every word, hoping that this time, a so-called apolitical renegade will deliver what they desperately need.

Equally frightening is the world view and political history of Vice President Mike Pence who would become President should there no longer be a President Trump. While Trump fits and sputters and tantrums on Twitter, Pence has coldly and carefully calculated a form of theocratic fascism that he may be salivating to install. Thus, we cannot fall back on a successor as a possible alternative to Trump's incipient fascism.

Oxford Professor James McDougall in his article "No, This Isn't The 1930s, But Yes, This Is Fascism," with reference to the election of Donald Trump writes:

> This is a new fascism, or at least near-fascism, and the centre right is dangerously underestimating its potential, exactly as it did 80 years ago. Then, it was conservative

anti-communists who believed they could tame and control the extremist fringe. Now, it is mainstream conservatives, facing little electoral challenge from a left in disarray. They fear the drift of their own voters to more muscular, anti-immigrant demagogues on the right. They accordingly espouse the right's priorities and accommodate its hate speech. They reassure everyone that they have things under control even as the post–Cold War neoliberal order, like the war-damaged bourgeois golden age last century, sinks under them.

The risk, at least for the West, is not a new world war, but merely a poisoned public life, a democracy reduced to the tyranny of tiny majorities who find emotional satisfaction in a violent, resentful rhetoric while their narrowly-elected leaders strip away their rights and persecute their neighbours.[44]

We are painfully aware that all-encompassing fascism in the twenty-first century will manifest differently than it has in the past, and this too is deeply troubling. We *must* resist because the consequences of twenty-first century fascism would be unimaginably horrific. Consider this: Unlike Germany's fascism of the 1930s, we possess today nuclear weapons, biological weapons, massive surveillance infrastructures, a gargantuan military industrial complex working hand in glove with transnational corporations of enormous power, a potentially servile media, and a populace that has been systematically undereducated and seduced into endless distraction. We have never experienced fascism on Earth in this context. When you contemplate soberly each of these dangers and then imagine them united under ruthless authoritarian control, what you see in your mind's eye are the lineaments of a Death Machine of horrific power, capable not only of creating a society of unparalleled brutality and dysfunction, but also of unconsciously serving Kali and destroying the Earth. Hitler in his wildest dreams of domination could not have imagined anything this all-encompassing. What is most chilling is that we can clearly see that all of these dangers are now waiting in the wings of history to congeal into a whirlwind of annihilation.

Hours after the Inauguration of Donald Trump, Occidental College Professor Peter Drier penned his article, "American Fascist," in which he stated that:

> The United States is not Weimar Germany. Our economic problems are nowhere as bad as those in Depression-era Germany. Nobody in the Trump administration (not even Steven Bannon) is calling for mass genocide (although saber-rattling with nuclear weapons could lead to global war if we're not careful).

> That said, it is useful for Americans to recognize that we are facing something entirely new and different in American history. Certainly none of us in our lifetimes have confronted an American government led by someone like Trump in terms of his sociopathic, demagogic, impulsive, and vindictive personality (not even Nixon came close). We've never seen a president with so little familiarity with the truth; he is a pathological liar, on matters large and small.

We are witnessing something new in terms of the uniformly right-wing inner circle with whom he's surrounded himself and appointed to his cabinet. We must adjust our thinking and view with alarm his reactionary and dangerous policy agenda on foreign policy, the economy, the environment, health care, immigration, civil liberties, and poverty. We have to be willing to sweep aside past presidential precedents in order to understand Trump's willingness to overtly invoke all the worst ethnic, religious, and racial hatreds in order to appeal to the most despicable elements of our society and unleash an upsurge of racism, anti-semitism, sexual assault, and nativism by the KKK and other hate groups. We need to suspend our textbook explanations about the American presidency in order to recognize Trump's ignorance about our Constitutional principles and the rule of law, and his lack of experience with collaboration and compromise.[45]

Five realities, we believe, facilitate a further descent into fascism:

The first is the death of conscience. We strongly believe that Donald Trump is a sociopathic narcissist. Please notice the word *believe* because it is unethical to diagnose someone one has never met or interviewed. Nevertheless, the indicators are very compelling as psychiatrist Robert Klitzman opined in his October, 2016 article "Trump and a Psychiatrist's Views of Sociopathy and Narcissism."[46] Perhaps the most distinct characteristic of a sociopath is that that individual lacks a conscience. Donald Trump has provided many indicators that he lacks a conscience, and one revelation of his presidential win is that collectively, our culture is speeding farther away from having a conscience. Increasingly, efforts to champion morality and decency are perceived as priggish and yes, "politically correct." Trump, the iconoclast, appealed to the maverick in his supporters and hooked their shadow by giving them permission to be racist, misogynist, xenophobic, and combative. When we understand this, we are no longer surprised by his victory. This death of conscience in our society is one of the indicators that Kali Yuga is in full sway. The ancient texts tell us that when cultures lose their ability to distinguish right from wrong, good from evil, the seeds of horrific collapse are already flowering.

The second is the death of facts. As noted above, the actual truth of what occurs is no longer relevant. Trump supporter and CNN Commentator, Scottie Nell Hughes, argued during his presidential campaign, "One thing that has been interesting this entire campaign season to watch is that people say facts are facts, but they're not really facts. Everybody has a way, it's kind of like looking at ratings or looking at a glass of half-full water. Everybody has a way of interpreting them to be the truth or not true."[47] Related to the death of conscience, the death of facts offers a blank check to lies as we have witnessed during the Trump campaign and the first several months of his administration. It appears that for Trump, lying is like breathing, and statements like, "I won by a landslide," or "I know more about ISIS than the generals do," have not only become commonplace but are eerily reminiscent of Orwell's *1984*. Again, the ancient texts regarding Kali Yuga inform us that when our political and spiritual leaders manipulate shamelessly through lies, and people respond cynically or slavishly, the end of civilization is near.

The third death is the death of any expectation of a sane and grounded leadership. During the past twenty years, we have been exposed to scandal after scandal that has shown us the dereliction of the gurus, the horrific sexual crimes of Catholic priests protected by a supine Vatican, the unbridled greed of a sordid regiment of CEOs, the depraved stupidity of celebrities imprisoned in mindless and brutal cults such as Scientology, and revelations of newspaper barons using their enormous wealth to spread disinformation about crucial issues such as climate change. This list could continue for the rest of the book, and what it suggests is a massive failure of leadership on all levels and the corrosion, by greed and lust for power, of all world institutions and elites. In such a situation those of us who long for sane and grounded leadership find ourselves bereft and shattered. Given what we now know, it would be ludicrous to expect this leadership from any of the traditional sources—our politicians, experts, pundits, the media, or religious leaders. As we have seen in Germany, China, and Cambodia, all of these can be comandeered and put into the service of totalitarian destruction. In the ancient Hindu texts regarding Kali Yuga, perhaps the most ominous sign of the end of civilization is that leaders with ethical responsibilities use their power only to enrich, dominate, and destroy.

The fourth death is the death of faith in humanity. Perhaps none of the deaths named above lends itself to the flowering of fascism as dramatically as the terrifying mistrust of humanity burgeoning around us. As many humans witness the horrors that our own species has visited upon the planet, ourselves, and other species, they are being seduced by the delusion of artificial intelligence. Chinese technology executive and computer scientist, Kai Fu Lee in his New York Times article, "The Real Threat of Artificial Intelligence," argues that:

> What is artificial intelligence today? Roughly speaking, it's technology that takes in huge amounts of information from a specific domain (say, loan repayment histories) and uses it to make a decision in a specific case (whether to give an individual a loan) in the service of a specified goal (maximizing profits for the lender). Think of a spreadsheet on steroids, trained on big data. These tools can outperform human beings at a given task.

> This kind of A.I. is spreading to thousands of domains (not just loans), and as it does, it will eliminate many jobs. Bank tellers, customer service representatives, telemarketers, stock and bond traders, even paralegals and radiologists will gradually be replaced by such software. Over time this technology will come to control semiautonomous and autonomous hardware like self-driving cars and robots, displacing factory workers, construction workers, drivers, delivery workers and many others.

> Unlike the Industrial Revolution and the computer revolution, the A.I. revolution is not taking certain jobs (artisans, personal assistants who use paper and typewriters) and replacing

> them with other jobs (assembly-line workers,
> personal assistants conversant with computers).
> Instead, it is poised to bring about a wide-scale
> decimation of jobs — mostly lower-paying jobs,
> but some higher-paying ones, too. [48]

The consequences of this, Lee notes, are twofold: Enormous amounts of money will be concentrated in the hands of the companies that develop A.I. at the same time that countless numbers of individuals will become permanently unemployed. Yet more tragic than the economic consequences is the concept of *singularity* that lies at the core of A.I.

In his 2017 article "Blind Spot," Peter Russell explains that singularity is "a point when equations break down and become meaningless." Proponents of singularity argue that if computing power keeps doubling every eighteen months, as it has done for the last fifty years, then sometime in the late 2020s there will be computers that equal the human brain in performance and abilities. From there it is only a small step to computers that can surpass the human brain. These ultra-intelligent machines could then be used to design even more intelligent computers. And do so faster."[49] According to Russell, singularity assumes that "the rate of development will continue to accelerate. Indeed, the emergence of ultra-intelligent machines will undoubtedly lead to a further explosion in acceleration. Within decades of passing the technological singularity, rates of change will become astronomical."[50] All of this, its proponents argue, leads to exponential growth which also leads to exponential stress—not only stress on the individual human being, but stress on all systems involved.

Russell emphasizes that, "A system can only tolerate so much stress; then it breaks down. If a wheel is made to spin faster and faster, it will eventually break apart under the stress. In a similar way as rates of change get ever-faster, the systems involved will reach a point where they too break apart. Whether it be our own biological system, social, economic, and political systems, or the planetary ecosystem, the stress of ever-increasing change will eventually lead to breakdown. Crises will pile upon each other faster and faster, heading us into the perfect global storm."[51]

The fifth death is the death of the sacred. Unfortunately, many activists have an understandable but profoundly limiting rejection of religion and any form of spirituality. This is extremely dangerous because only an activism grounded in a spiritual perspective and rooted in simple but galvanizing spiritual practices can possibly be both effective and sufficiently persistent in this exploding crisis. One of our deepest purposes in writing this book is to awaken activists of every kind to the urgent necessity of empowering themselves at a far deeper level than they are doing now, with the peace, passion, stamina and moral and spiritual strength that can only come from an incessant cultivation of the inner divine. Gandhi could never have been effective in overturning the British Empire without the spiritual depth of his whole enterprise. Martin Luther King, Jr. could never have prevented a racist bloodbath without appealing to the nobility of Christ consciousness. Lech Walesa would never have made _solidarnosc_ into such a powerful transforming force without constantly invoking the devotion most Poles have to the Black Madonna. The Dalai Lama's tireless advocacy for compassion and harmony would be far less powerful if were not grounded in Buddhist awakening. Most recently, the extraordinary manifestation of courage and truth-telling that blazed from the Standing Rock resistance would not have been possible without the grounding of that resistance in constant ritual, prayer, and meditation. It would be tragic if the dominant soulless culture prevents activists from drawing on the grace, power, stamina, strength and discerning wisdom of the conscious spirit. We believe that confronting the appallingly difficult world crisis in which we are engulfed without being sustained by spiritual practice is, as Marion Woodman once said to Andrew, like walking into a raging forest fire dressed only in a paper tutu.

When you dare to contemplate and absorb the brutal impact of these five deaths, it will become clear that the reconnection we are calling for cannot be static. To reconnect with Self, with other, and with Earth is not the sentimental feeling-orgy that the New Age loves to celebrate. Reconnecting with the Self reveals clearly the tyranny and illusion of the false self. Reconnecting with other in authentic compassion reveals all the structures of prejudice and oppression that demonize or destroy the other. Reconnecting with Earth in its glory and fecund sacredness unveils starkly the horror of what we are doing to animals and ecosystems everywhere. Reconnection then, inevitably brings with it the necessity of resistance on every level with all of its responsibilities of discernment, discipline, and unyielding emphasis on justice.

In his extraordinary masterpiece, *The Order-Disorder Paradox: Understanding The Hidden Side of Change In Self and Society*[52], Nathan Schwartz-Salant offers us a vision grounded in science, transpersonal psychology, and the mystical traditions of how any new order inevitably creates chaos. This chaos, even when extreme, does not have to be approached with paralysis and despair if we create a container strong, spacious, and lucid enough to be able to weather it and watch for the signs of the order it could potentially give birth to and continue to work inwardly and outwardly for the new possibilities that will be visible if we develop the eyes to perceive them.

What this demands of us is an unprecedented claiming of our own inner and outer authority. If humanity is going to have a ghost of a chance of avoiding the lethal stage of Kali's dance, it can only be through the arising of a worldwide movement of universal love in action. This cannot come from above. That much must be obvious to any sane person. It can only come from the individual acts of millions of ordinary people daring to come together in what will inevitably be increasingly dangerous circumstances to claim and take back their power. In an increasingly authoritarian society, where all the authorities without exception are corrupt, the only source of strength is within ourselves and within the communities we improvise and create. This must be squarely faced in order for any possibility of transformation to occur. Furthermore, this is extremely difficult to achieve in a situation that will include growing chaos and terror. This is why deep inner and outer work are demanded of all of us in order to give us the tools with which to prepare for what will inevitably be a bloody and costly struggle in darkening conditions.

Resistance

In a variety of ways, Donald Trump has violated the US Constitution since taking office. His global business ties allow him to enrich himself financially while holding the office of President of The United States, a situation clearly prohibited by the emoluments clause of the Constitution. Moreover, his travel ban on individuals entering the United States from specific Middle Eastern countries has been deemed unconstitutional by several courts. In addition, Trump's firing of FBI Director James Comey, who was in charge of investigating Russian meddling in the 2016 election and a possible Russian collusion with the Trump campaign, threatens our democracy. He also issued an Executive Order that seeks to cut off funding to sanctuary cities where police do not ask citizens about their immigration status. Even more chilling is the reality that former White House Chief of Staff, Reince Preibus admitted that Trump and his inner circle have considered and *continue to consider* amending or even abolishing the First Amendment of the Constitution because of critical press coverage of President Trump. [53]

Throughout 2017 the Trump Administration has been surrounded by Congressional investigations regarding the meddling of Russia in the 2016 US elections, as well as increasing evidence of money laundering activity by and through Trump's business empire. Journalist, Craig Unger, writes in his July, 2017 New Republic article, "Trump's Russian Laundromat," that Trump Tower and other luxury high-rises have been used by Trump's empire to clean dirty money, run an international crime syndicate, and propel a failed real estate developer into the White

House. [54] Indications of deep financial and political ties with Vladimir Putin and the Russian government raise disturbing questions, including the possibility that Donald Trump has committed treason, a clearly criminal and impeachable offense.

While these are appalling crimes against the US Constitution and the people of the United States, the Trump Administration is committing and seeks to further commit crimes against the Earth. Jim Garrison, Founder and President of Ubiquity University notes that "Trump colluded with Putin to gain the presidency. That was a crime against the American people and the U.S. Constitution. Trump is now colluding with Putin and Exxon Oil to bring on the pipelines and drill for oil in the Arctic. This is a crime against humanity and against Nature. It will tip climate change into irreversibility."[55] A 2016 CNBC article, "Exxon Mobil could tap huge Arctic assets if US-Russian relations thaw," explains that "Exxon Mobil stands to regain access to huge reserves of oil if the United States rolls back sanctions on Russia." [56] While some climate scientists believe that the extinction of life on Earth is already certain, Arctic drilling and associated pipelines in the Arctic would make the elimination of all living beings on this planet a *fait accompli*.

In the first six months of the Trump Administration, it appears that his blatant, unambiguous steering of the United States in the direction of fascism has been tempered by neoliberal, globalist forces surrounding him—forces that have maintained power over Presidential administrations in the United States since the end of World War II. Trump clearly assumed he could ride into Washington and rule in the manner to which he is accustomed after decades of managing his own business empire. He assumed that he could surround himself with associates who held a similar renegade perspective, but in fact, he was required to appoint some "adults" to cabinet positions, and with their expertise came the traditional neoliberal perspective which compelled Trump to adapt. Thus, within the first 100 days, we witnessed a host of "unexplainable" pivots in his position on a variety of issues—not unexplainable, however, if one understands the underlying world view of the Washington establishment. At the same time, however, Trump's cabinet is replete with millionaires and billionaires and outspoken deniers of climate change. What is more, as investigations of Trump's likely illegal and possibly treasonous financial ties with Russia persevere, he demonstrates an unflinching adherence to authoritarian rule, demanding uncompromising personal and political loyalty.

Consequently, what must now be resisted is not so much jackbooted authoritarianism as an unbridled and unabashed attack on the environment, massive transfers of wealth from the middle class and working poor, and the privatization of public institutions and services. Each of these is a tentacle issuing from the torso of a gargantuan economic system which Naomi Klein names "Disaster Capitalism."[57]

We believe the current scandals and investigations that essentially inhibit the functioning of government in current time will only deepen and intensify. The Trump Administration appears to be ensnared in a self-created and self-destructive meltdown of its own making. On the one hand, we may cheer, yet as noted above, the defeat of Trump will have little effect on our predicament because we cannot impeach our way out of fascism or the potential extinction that threatens every living being on Earth.

It is now time to become adults and engage in a no-nonsense plan of resistance going forward. While the need for reconnection will be continuous for the rest of our lives, anyone who seriously contemplates what could lie ahead will realize that the forms and modes of resistance will need to be constantly adapted to whatever occurs. This will demand both an unprecedented inner discipline and an unprecedented suppleness and flexibility of approach, in other words, resilience. The resistance to which we are summoning you cannot be satisfied with minor victories, given the extent of the crisis. It is a resistance to which those who understand our predicament must make a lifelong commitment and be willing to pay any price to keep resistance alive, because any human future depends on it.

Decolonizing and Detoxifying

In his 2012 article, *Unsettling Ourselves*, Derrick Jensen quotes the Osage Chief, Big Soldier, who said of the dominant culture, "I see and admire your manner of living. . . . In short you can do almost what you choose. You whites possess the power of subduing almost every animal to your use. You are surrounded by slaves. Everything about you is in chains and you are slaves yourselves. I fear that if I should exchange my pursuits for yours, I too should become a slave."[58]

Jensen then comments, "The essence of the dominant culture, of civilization, is slavery. It is based on slavery, and it requires slavery. It attempts to enslave the land, to enslave nonhumans, and to enslave humans. It attempts to get us all to believe that all relationships are based on slavery, based on domination, such that humans dominate the land and everyone who lives on it, men dominate women, whites dominate non-whites, the civilized dominate everyone. And overarching everyone is civilization—the system itself. We are taught to believe that the system—civilization—is more important than life on earth."[59] Furthermore, he argues that civilization is a disease that kills the land and kills those who live with the land; it is also an addiction, and addictions turn people into slaves.

But how do we de-colonize ourselves? How do we heal our disease and recover from our addiction? Jensen answers:

> Decolonization is the process of breaking your identity with and loyalty to this culture—industrial capitalism, and more broadly civilization—and remembering your identification with and loyalty to the real physical world, including the land where you live. It means re-examining premises and stories the dominant culture handed down to you. It means seeing the harm the dominant culture does to other cultures, and to the planet. If you are a member of settler society, it means recognizing that you are living on stolen land and it means working to return that land to the humans whose blood has forever mixed with the soil. If you are an indigenous person it means never forgetting that your land was stolen, and it means working to repossess that land, and it means working to be repossessed by that land. It means recognizing that the luxuries of the dominant culture do not come free, but rather are paid for by

other humans, by nonhumans, by the whole world. It means recognizing that we do not live in a functioning democracy, but rather in a corporate plutocracy, a government by, for, and of corporations. Decolonization means internalizing the implications of that. It means recognizing that neither technological progress nor increased GNP is good for the planet. It means recognizing that the dominant culture is not good for the planet. Decolonization means internalizing the implications of the fact that the dominant culture is killing the planet. It means determining that we will stop this culture from doing that. It means determining that we will not fail. It means remembering that the real world is more important than this social system: without a real world you don't have a social system, any social system. All of this is the barest beginnings of decolonizing. It is internal work that doesn't accomplish anything in the real world, but makes all further steps more likely, more feasible, and in many ways more strictly technical.[60]

Decolonizing ourselves is an act of resistance initiated from the inside and the source of all authentic resistance externally. External resistance is essential, but it is pointless until we have decolonized ourselves from the inside out. Given how long our colonization has taken and how deeply ingrained its values are in the psyche, decolonization is a long, perhaps *life*-long process to which we must commit with patience, perseverance, and compassion for ourselves, but also ruthless commitment. External resistance to enslavement is another form of dangerous hypocrisy if we do not also resist our emotional and spiritual enslavement.

The first step in decolonizing ourselves is to examine and heal the shadow. As defined above, the shadow is any part of us that does not fit with our ego image of ourselves and which we therefore unconsciously disown. Shadow material remains unconscious but does not vanish. In fact, the more we repress it, the more it demands our attention and does so by erupting in our lives and our relationships unpredictably and quite inconveniently.

As we commit to doing rigorous shadow healing, we increasingly detoxify from the colonizing messages the culture sends us daily and hourly. Shadow healing allows us to recognize them early on and resist them with discernment and grace. With practice, we develop finely-tuned "deception detectors" in the psyche that inhibit further colonization.

It is now painfully obvious that old forms of resistance will not serve us. In addition to our commitment to shadow healing, we must understand that the unprecedentedly toxic predicament in which we are steeped demands the development and deployment of a new *kind* of resistor. We call this the Warrior/Midwife within the psyche that enables us to resist the toxic messages of the culture at the same time that we give birth to an embodied, sacred humanity—both our own humanity and that of other members of our species. As a Warrior, regardless of our gender, we are wed to the sacred masculine which empowers us to develop the capacity to discern, undermine, and resist the malignancy of social and political oppression. As a Midwife, we are wed to the sacred feminine which allows us to birth unimaginable compassion, tenderness, vulnerability, and magnanimity as well as an extraordinary ability to remain humbly open and supple to guidance. Both the Warrior and Midwife must be increasingly refined and united in anyone who chooses to literally, physically rebel against an authoritarian order that carries the horrific power that is now possible.

Rising Up

The day after the Inauguration of Donald Trump, Chris Hedges gave a speech at the "Inaugurate Resistance" rally in Washington, DC, entitled "Revolt Is the Only Barrier to a Fascist America." A few highlights from the speech demand our attention:

- We are entering the twilight phase of capitalism. Wealth is no longer created by producing or manufacturing. It is created by manipulating the prices of stocks and commodities and imposing a crippling debt peonage on the public. Our casino capitalism has merged with the gambling industry. The entire system is parasitic. It is designed to prey on the desperate—young men and women burdened by student loans, underpaid workers burdened by credit card debt and mortgages, towns and cities forced to borrow to maintain municipal services.
- When a tiny cabal seizes power—monarchist, communist, fascist or corporate—it creates a mafia economy and a mafia state. Donald Trump is not an anomaly. He is the grotesque visage of a collapsed democracy.
- What comes next, history has shown, will not be pleasant. A corrupt and inept ruling elite, backed

by the organs of state security and law enforcement, will unleash a naked kleptocracy. Workers will become serfs. The most benign dissent will be criminalized. The ravaging of the ecosystem propels us towards extinction. Hate talk will call for attacks against Muslims, undocumented workers, African-Americans, feminists, intellectuals, artists and dissidents, all of whom will be scapegoated for the country's stagnation. Magical thinking will dominate our airwaves and be taught in our public schools. Art and culture will be degraded to nationalist kitsch. All the cultural and intellectual disciplines that allow us to view the world from the perspective of the other, that foster empathy, understanding, and compassion will be replaced by a grotesque and cruel hyper-masculinity and hyper-militarism. Those in power will validate racism, bigotry, misogyny and homophobia.

- Revolt is a political necessity. It is a moral imperative. It is a defense of the sacred. It allows us to live in truth. It alone makes hope possible.

- I do not know if we can build a better society. I do not even know if we will survive as a species. But I do know these corporate forces have us by the throat. And they have my children by the throat. I do not fight fascists because I will win. I fight fascists because they are fascists.[61]

As we have previously stated, our preference lies eternally and wholeheartedly with non-violent resistance, but in the severe stage of oppression, we must face the reality that the only possible dignified option may be violent resistance. Paradoxically however, only those who have trained in non-violence could possibly be counted on to employ violence with some semblance of restraint and only as a last resort. We do not acknowledge this lightly.

In no way do we justify violent tactics because we believe that the focus and action of our resistance must remain non-violent. The danger we see in some activist circles is that violence is in fashion which prevents a deep training in non-violence and assures a tragic outcome not only in terms of loss of life, but also in terms of effectiveness.

In his essential and masterful book, *The Wages of Rebellion: The Moral Imperative of Revolt*, Chris Hedges explores "the personal cost of rebellion—what it takes emotionally, psychologically, and physically to defy absolute power." Hedges emphasizes the passion that drives the rebel:

> Rebels share much in common with religious mystics. They hold fast to a vision that often they alone can see. They view rebellion as a moral imperative, even as they concede that the hope of success is slim and at times impossible. . . . The best of them are driven by a profound empathy, even love for the vulnerable, the persecuted, and the weak.[62]

Anyone choosing to follow a spiritual path and adhere to the values of love and compassion will constantly be confronted with difficult decisions about how to survive and yet remain moral beings. Given the trauma and horror that the rebel may have to face, it is virtually impossible to determine ahead of time what they will have to endure or what choices they may be forced to make. What *is* certain is that without astringent decolonization and detoxification from the values of the dominant culture and without rigorous Warrior/Midwife training and practice, the rebel is likely to be destroyed from within as well as from without.

What then does the descent from a non-violent to a violent scenario look like? Hedges answers by observing:

> If a nonviolent popular movement is able to ideologically disarm the bureaucrats, civil servants, and police—to get them, in essence to defect—nonviolent revolution is possible. But if the state can organize effective and prolonged violence against dissent, then state violence can spawn reactive revolutionary violence, or what the state calls "terrorism." Violent uprisings are always tragic, and violent revolutions always empower revolutionaries, such as Lenin and the Bolsheviks, who are as ruthless as their adversaries. Violence inevitably becomes the principal form of coercion on both sides of the divide. Social upheaval without clear definition and direction, without ideas behind it, swiftly descends into nihilism, terrorism, and chaos. It consumes itself. This is the minefield we will have to cross.[63]

We shudder to contemplate that this kind of scenario could lie ahead of us or our descendants in the coming years, yet whatever form resistance takes, it must include at least two elements without which it cannot prevail.

The first is a *spiritual foundation* that may have nothing to do with religion but that is grounded in something larger and more profound than the human ego. Whether Standing Rock, the American civil rights movement, Gandhi's freedom struggle, or Nelson Mandela's anti-apartheid resistance movement, all possessed some aspect of emotional and spiritual intelligence that compelled and sustained their efforts. Even those who identify as atheist by their very dedication to a cause are walking a "spiritual" path by virtue of their dedication to something greater than themselves.

Secondly, we cannot resist in isolation or without the *support of other resistors.* This is precisely why in his blueprint for Sacred Activism, Andrew created Networks of Grace—a massive grassroots mobilization of the hearts and committed wills of millions of people. He explains that, "From my study of terrorist and fundamentalist organizations I had learned one essential thing—that the success of their movements relies on cells—small individual cells of between six and twelve people—who encourage, sustain, and inspire each other with sacred reading and meditation and who share each other's victories and defeats in the course of what they believe is sacred action."[64]

All groups of resistors in all cultures have sustained each other through music, poetry, art, and dance. Likewise ceremony and community rituals have galvanized groups to endure what would otherwise become unbearable. "Rebellion requires empathy and love," writes Chris Hedges. "It requires self-sacrifice. It requires the honoring of the sacred."[65]

Strategies of Resistance

In his brilliant article, "How to Build an Autocracy," David Frum notes that asking whether or not Trump is a fascist is actually the wrong question. Frum states that, "Perhaps the better question about Trump is not 'What is he?' but 'What will he do to us'?"[66] What he will do, Frum argues, depends a great deal, literally, on how much he can get away with in a culture that has become dumbed-down, desperate, and demoralized. Frum warns us to be vigilant with respect to cultural disregards for the rule of law and the "flouting of rules that bind everyone else." Perhaps the most stunning example of this is acceptance by the culture of Trump's refusal to reveal his tax returns. Witnessing his *modus operandi* from afar, one sees a classic textbook model of a professional con artist mesmerizing and deceiving his victim.

Frum insists that "What happens in the next four years will depend heavily on whether Trump is right or wrong about how little Americans care about their democracy and the habits and conventions that sustain it. If they surprise him, they can restrain him." Thus, it is crucial that we remain awake and struggle continually to find ways to reach out to and awaken others as long as it is possible to do so.

We must also be shrewd in our strategies of resistance because Trump being Trump is likely to manipulate protest for his own ends. Frum notes that, "Civil unrest will not be a problem for the Trump presidency. It will be a resource. Trump will likely want not to repress it, but to publicize it—and the conservative entertainment-outrage complex will eagerly assist him. Immigration protesters marching with Mexican flags; Black Lives Matter demonstrators bearing antipolice slogans—these are the images of the opposition that Trump will wish his supporters to see. The more offensively the protesters behave, the more pleased Trump will be."[67]

Frum confronts us with a clear, no-nonsense challenge:

> [T]he way that liberty must be defended is not with amateur firearms, but with an unwearying insistence upon the honesty, integrity, and professionalism of American institutions and those who lead them. We are living through the most dangerous challenge to the free government of the United States that anyone alive has encountered. What happens next is up to you and me. Don't be afraid. This moment of danger can also be your finest hour as a citizen and an American.[68]

Without using the words or perhaps even having a clear notion of the concept, Frum is essentially asking us to be "wise as serpents and harmless as doves" in our resistance. He's admonishing us to resist, but to do so in ways that will not feed into the Trump agenda or Trump's fragile but volatile psyche. What he notes as absolutely essential-- honesty, integrity, ethical responsibility, and professionalism, will be daunting to demand in an era of "alternative facts" and tolerance for flagrant, unvarnished lying.

In his March, 2017 article "Containing Trump," Jonathan Rauch, echoing the perspective of his *Atlantic* colleague, David Frum, argues that throughout America's history, some presidents have demonstrated renegade, autocratic tendencies, but were contained by media, public opinion, and various forms of resistance. "Whether any particular presidential action, or pattern of action, is authoritarian thus depends not just on the action itself but on how everyone else responds to it," says Rauch.[69] He is encouraged by the burgeoning resistance he sees everywhere in America, but also adds:

> If you think it's ridiculous to imagine that one nascent group, or even a handful of heavy hitters like the ACLU, could shift the orbit of Planet Trump, you're right. The point is that a civil-society mobilization involves multitudes of groups and people forming a whole greater than the sum of its parts.[70]

Rauch asserts that if we stay true to the perspective of the Founding Fathers, we will be able to contain Trump. "To help the body politic resist de-norming," states Rauch, "you need to make an argument for the kind of government and society that the norms support. You have to explain why lying, bullying, and coarsening are the enemies of the kinds of lives people aspire to. Instead of pointing to Trump with shock and disgust—tactics that seem to help more than hurt him—you need to offer something better. In other words, you need to emulate what the Founders did so many years ago, when they offered, and then built, a more perfect union."[71]

Clearly, we are witnessing a groundswell of activism unseen in American culture since the late 1960s. The day after Trump's inauguration brought forth perhaps the largest demonstration in human history. On that day, millions of women around the globe took to the streets to protest his policies with respect to women's rights and services. This historic protest was followed by protests on behalf of science and against climate change denial and shortly thereafter, a peoples' climate march specifically demanding United States government action on climate change. Moreover, unprecedented numbers of constituents turned out throughout America as members of Congress held town hall meetings to discuss the repeal of Obamacare. In a manner not seen since perhaps pre–Revolutionary War America, citizens passionately shouted down their senators and representatives, declaring their disgust with the new administration's policies.

This historic increase in activism is refreshing, moving, and inspiring, but it needs a structure and a strategy so that it can sink its roots into the soil of resistance; we must demand systemic change rather than resigning ourselves to single-issue protests. The great danger of the current kind of resistance we are witnessing is that it may not come together in a united force and it may—through inner dissension or careless, violent action—play directly into the hands of the forces in power ready to destroy it.

Nevertheless, a fierce, tenacious, and substantive form of activism was demonstrated in July, 2017 when the Republican effort to repeal and replace Obamacare was defeated in the US Senate. While the deciding "no" votes were cast by Senators McCain, Murkowski, and Collins, their votes, along with other "no" votes in the Senate were significantly driven by the mobilization of thousands of disabled individuals and individuals undergoing treatment for severe or terminal illnesses who would have lost their healthcare had Congress voted to repeal and replace Obamacare.

Following the defeat of the repeal and replace legislation, the Common Dreams website championed ADAPT (Americans Disabled Attendant Programs Today)--a national organization that engages in nonviolent civil disobedience to protect the rights of the disabled. Staff writer Jake Johnson emphasized that, "Throughout the Trumpcare fight, ADAPT activists played a central role; for weeks they occupied Senate offices overnight, faced arrest, and in some cases endured harsh treatment from law enforcement to highlight the devastating effects Trumpcare would have on America's most vulnerable."[72]

As elders who are still able-bodied, we have to ask ourselves if we would be prepared to go to such heroic lengths? If the disabled and most vulnerable can affect such shocking change through sheer courage, what does that say about the rest of us? We must be worthy, if we can be, of their challenge.

We are not professional organizers or seasoned political resisters. Others more experienced than we are in resistance movements have developed a variety of strategies. However, we wish to offer a few fundamental concepts from *This Is an Uprising: How Nonviolent Revolt Is Shaping the Twenty-First Century*, by Mark and Paul Engler. After extensive research on nonviolent movements throughout the twentieth century, the Englers examine how to construct and sustain incidents of widespread protest in order to create and sustain transformation.

This Is an Uprising offers a fascinating exploration of a variety of protest strategies with emphasis on two different perspectives on grassroots action. One is that of the famous organizer, Saul Alinsky, often regarded as the founding father of community organizing. The other perspective is that of Frances Fox Piven, welfare rights sociologist and campaigner for voting rights.

Alinsky was a mentor in the art of the slow, incremental building of community groups, similar to labor organizing which focused on person-by-person recruitment and strategic leadership development. Conversely, Piven was a guru of unruly, broad-based disobedience that emphasized the "disruptive power of mass mobilizations that coalesce quickly, draw in participants not previously involved in organizing, and leave established elites scrambling to adjust to a new political landscape."[73]

Engler and Engler do not favor one approach or the other but emphasize the importance of each. They summarize that, "The future of social change in this country may well involve integrating these approaches—figuring out how the strengths of both structure and mass protest can be used in tandem—so that outbreaks of widespread revolt complement long-term organizing."[74] According to the authors, some situations call for the Alinsky approach which they name *transactional*, whereas in other situations, the Piven or *transformational* approach is more appropriate. Whereas the transactional strategy seeks to build individual relationships, the transformational strategy seeks to influence the public at large. However, it is important to understand that these two approaches are not written in stone, nor should we assume that never shall the two meet or that the strategic use of both at different times and on different occasions is forbidden.

For example, when one is organizing a labor strike,

which is almost always a protracted struggle, the Alinsky approach is appropriate, but when responding to a sudden pronouncement or executive order from the President of the United States, the Piven strategy is necessary. The worldwide women's marches of January, 2017 and the nationwide protests against Donald Trump's travel ban targeting immigrants from seven Muslim countries one week after his inauguration are specific examples of the latter.

The authors also emphasize that the three elements of *disruption, sacrifice*, and *escalation* are crucial to understand and strategically implement in the overall protest process. In other words, organizers must assess the extent of the societal disruption they are willing to create and the value it will have or not have in terms of influencing public opinion in favor of the protestors' cause. Moreover, protestors must assess the level of sacrifice they are willing to make in terms of personal risk, financial risk, loss of employment or other losses resulting from their efforts. Additionally, organizers often discover that their first efforts are minimally effective or barely noticed. They must then assess whether they wish to escalate and the risks involved in doing so. Often escalating the frequency and intensity of their protest actions is necessary in order to galvanize public support on their behalf. In other situations, escalation could potentially harm their efforts or shatter them altogether. At all times, the movement must be focused on public support, and they "tend to succeed when they win over ever-greater levels of public support for their cause and undermine the pillars of support for the opposition."[75]

In their book, the Englers devote a significant amount of attention to the Occupy Wall Street movement, birthed in 2011—a movement comprised of individuals who aspired to nothing less than a revolutionary shift in America's economic structure. The authors analyze some of Occupy's shortcomings but conclude, "Yet despite its lack of institutional backing, it accomplished precisely what far more muscular organizations had tried and failed, to do in the years before. Its mixture of disruption, sacrifice, and escalation ended up having concrete implications, both small and large."[76] Out of many years' experience and the Occupy Movement, the Englers launched their powerful Momentum Training program which takes social justice organizing to an entirely new level. [77] We also recommend the Englers' 2017 "Resistance Guide" which can be read at https://guidingtheresistance.com/.

Engler and Engler conclude:

> Along the way, a variety of key lessons have emerged. Momentum-driven organizing uses the tools of civil resistance to consciously spark, amplify, and harness mass protest. . . .[It wins] by swaying public opinion and pulling the pillars of support. . . . It uses disruption, sacrifice, and escalation to build tension and bring overlooked issues into the public spotlight. It aspires, at its peak, to create moments of the whirlwind, when outbreaks of decentralized action extend far outside the institutional limits of any one organization. It is willing to polarize public opinion and risk controversy with bold protests, but it maintains nonviolent discipline to ensure that it does not undermine broad-based support for its cause. . . . The point of momentum-driven organizing

is not to deny the contributions of other approaches. But it is to suggest a simple and urgent idea: that uprising can be a craft, and that this craft can change our world.[78]

In his January, 2017 article "American Psychosis," on his *Truthdig* blog, Chris Hedges wrote:

> We are entering a period of national psychological trauma. We are stalked by lunatics. We are, as Judith Herman writes about trauma victims in her book "Trauma and Recovery: The Aftermath of Violence—From Domestic Abuse to Political Terror," being "rendered helpless by overwhelming force." This trauma, like all traumas, overwhelms "the ordinary systems of care that give people a sense of control, connection, and meaning." To recover our mental balance we must respond to Trump the way victims of trauma respond to abuse. We must build communities where we can find understanding and solidarity. We must allow ourselves to mourn. We must name the psychosis that afflicts us. We must carry out acts of civil disobedience and steadfast defiance to re-empower others and ourselves. We must fend off the madness and engage in dialogues based on truth, literacy, empathy and reality. We must invest more time in activities such as finding solace in nature, or focusing on music, theater, literature, art and even worship—activities that hold the capacity for renewal and transcendence. This is the only way we will remain psychologically whole.

Building an outer shell or attempting to hide
will exacerbate our psychological distress and
depression. We may not win, but we will have,
if we create small, like-minded cells of defiance,
the capacity not to go insane.[79]

While we honor the perspectives of Chris Hedges,
David Frum, Jonathan Rauch, and the Englers, we are also
painfully aware that a host of other factors may curtail or
impede even the most astute and brilliantly strategized forms
of resistance. One of the most troubling factors is that with
the Trump presidency, we have entered an Orwellian-like era
of "alternative facts" and "the death of facts," as noted above,
which promote the stupefying notion that truth is true when
one wants it to be true and untrue when one chooses not to
confront the truth. In this milieu, the architects of autocracy
have little concern for history, research, documentation, or
fact-checking. Rauch's suggestion that ". . . you need to
emulate what the Founders did so many years ago, when
they offered, and then built, a more perfect union" may
prove to be a futile endeavor in a dumbed-down culture that
no longer values reason or critical thinking but is frantically
devoted to the iconoclastic demolition of government itself.

Yet even if this ghastly erosion of reason were not
occurring in the culture, climate catastrophe and economic
chaos are two possible factors that will undermine our
capacity to resist as well as undermine our resistance efforts.
Nevertheless, as Sacred Activists, we understand that our
commitment to activism is never entirely about outcome,
but about taking actions that our hearts and souls demand
we take in the moment and surrendering the outcome to
the divine. What is more, only our reconnection with the

Self, with each other, and with Earth can sustain us in what appears to be the most daunting activist endeavor humans have ever known.

It is crucial for every activist to understand that they cannot resist by themselves in isolation and that in addition to being supported externally by their allies, they must be sustained internally by their deep connection and reconnection with the Self.

In *No Is Not Enough*, Naomi Klein reiterates her familiar "shock doctrine" theory so pervasive in what she calls "disaster capitalism." The shock doctrine is a theory for explaining the way that force, stealth and crises are used in implementing neoliberal economic policies such as privatization, deregulation and cuts to social services. She argues that the attacks of September 11, 2001 provided an ideal national, cultural, and political shock that allowed the creation of the War on Terror and led to unprecedented curtailments of civil liberties in the United States by way of the USA Patriot Act. In other words, contrived, human-made events often facilitate the forceful implementation of policies that would be rejected under normal circumstances.

Yet these events alone do not send us into a state of shock, Klein notes. "...it has to be something big and bad *that we do not yet understand.* A state of shock is what results when a gap opens up between events and our initial ability to explain them. When we find ourselves in the position, without a story, without our moorings, a great many people become vulnerable to authority figures telling us to fear one another and relinquish our rights for the greater good."[80] Taking this notion further, Klein writes:

...these tactics can be resisted. To do so, two crucial things have to happen. First, we need a firm grasp on how shock politics work and whose interests they serve. That understanding is how we get out of shock quickly and start fighting back. Second, and equally important, we have to tell a *different story* from the one the shock doctors are peddling, a vision of the world compelling enough to compete head-to-head with theirs. This value-based vision must offer a different path, away from serial shocks—one based on coming together across racial, ethnic, religious, and gender divides, rather than being wrenched further apart, and one based on healing the planet rather than unleashing further destabilizing wars and pollution. Most of all, that vision needs to offer those who are hurting—for lack of jobs, lack of health care, lack of peace, lack of hope—a tangibly better life.[81]

Klein's language at this juncture is indeed spiritual. Without deep connection with the sacred Self, other, and Earth, it is impossible to create a new story. It is precisely our lack of story---our lack of a shared commitment to a vision of connection and compassion that has allowed the rise to power of the shock doctors in the first place and prevents us from recovering from and resisting their shocks.

Reconnection and Resilience Alongside Resistance

Our emphasis in Chapter One was on Reconnection—with Self, others, and Earth. It is essential we understand that as we resist, we must continually nurture the connection with Self in myriad ways, and this particular form of reconnection influences our relationships with others and Earth.

As Sacred Activists, we must attend to our emotional landscape and as our friend Miriam Greenspan writes, "befriend the dark emotions." Often activists resist doing grief work or even approaching the topic at all because they believe that feeling their grief will cause them to become too vulnerable for engaging robustly in their activism. In fact, the opposite is true. As Andrew writes in *The Hope: A Guide to Sacred Activism,* the most authentic activism is an activism that originates in our own heartbreak over a particular type of suffering that compels us to take action to alleviate it. The capacity to engage passionately as activists while holding grief, anger, fear, and a host of other emotions in our hearts is what constitutes radical reconnection. Of course, we cannot do this without the support of allies who welcome our grief and champion our courage in expressing it. What is more, the Earth itself provides literally rock solid support for grieving activists, and at the end of this chapter in the Suggested Practices section, we offer a specific exercise for allowing the Earth to support us in grieving.

The importance of grief work for activists cannot be overemphasized. Activism issues from the fire in our bellies to engage socially, politically, economically, and on myriad levels to create radical change. Any activist reading these words understands on a cellular level the amount of energy and stamina activism requires. If grief work is avoided, the fires of our activism will invariably consume us, causing us to burn out. That fire must be tempered with the water of our tears so that we can remain tenacious yet tender in our struggles.

Attending to our emotional landscape at the same time we are engaged in resistance is crucial in order to cultivate the resilience required, not only to persevere but to maintain within ourselves the quality of life for which we are ultimately struggling. One aspect of our colonization that has brought us to the predicament in which we find ourselves is the minimizing of our inner life. If we ignore or underestimate the importance of our inner world in the process of toiling for the transformation of the outer world, we cannot possibly succeed because the "new" world is not likely to look different from the old. Activists limited by their colonization will be hard-pressed not only to resist skillfully but also to create a new culture of conscious human beings.

Suggested Practices

**When you hear the word *fascism*, what comes to mind, and what do you feel? Journal about this, and notice what happens as you allow yourself to explore the topic.

**Revisit Kali Holloway's article on the ways that Trump conforms to Umberto Eco's 14 points of fascism. You can find the online location in the footnotes of this book. Journal your thoughts and feelings about this resemblance.

**Notice the comments in this chapter by Derrick Jensen on colonization. You may want to read his entire article, "Unsettling Ourselves." You can find it online by Googling or by locating the link to the article in the footnotes of this book. What are some ways you feel you have been "colonized"? What steps are you taking to UN-colonize yourself?

**What do you know about your shadow? What work have you done toward healing the shadow? A very important tool which includes specific practices is Carolyn's book *Dark Gold: The Human Shadow and the Global Crisis.*

**Are you currently engaged in any form(s) of activism? If not, are there any forms of activism that call you? Whether or not you are engaged in activism, after reading this chapter, are there any aspects of your inner life that you would like to attend to?

**Re-read the excerpt from Chris Hedges' article, "American Psychosis." In it, he emphasizes that we must not only resist, but we must engage in activities that help us feel whole and energized. What are some activities that bring you "renewal and transcendence"?

**Do you allow yourself to feel the grief of our planetary predicament? If not, what stops you? If you do allow yourself to feel grief, what support systems do you have in place for doing that work? What additional forms of support might you need?

Chapter 3

Living Resiliently Amid Global Psychosis

To be resilient means to be able to 'spring back' into shape after being deformed. To be emotionally resilient means to be able to spring back emotionally after suffering through difficult and stressful times in one's life. Stressed people experience a flood of powerful negative emotions which may include anger, anxiety, and depression. Some people remain trapped in these negative emotions long after the stressful events that have caused them have passed. Emotionally resilient people, on the other hand, are quickly able to bounce back to their normal emotional state.

—"Defining Resilience," Harry Mills and
Mark Dombeck, Gracepoint Wellness[82]

We must never forget that we may also find meaning in life even when confronted with a hopeless situation, when facing a fate that cannot be changed. For what then matters is to bear witness to the uniquely human potential at its best, which is to transform a personal

> *tragedy into triumph, to turn one's predicament into a*
> *human achievement. When we are no longer able to change*
> *a situation—just think of an incurable disease such as*
> *inoperable cancer—we are challenged to change ourselves.*
> —Victor Frankl, *Man's Search for Meaning*[83]

In his article noted above, Chris Hedges speaks of "American Psychosis," and yet, it feels as if all industrially civilized countries are afflicted with epidemic madness, especially as eco and all other systems unravel.

Portland author, artist, and activist, Paul Levy asks, "Why Don't We See Our Collective Madness?" and answers:

> The major obstacle blocking people from seeing the collective psychosis that has afflicted our species is our unwillingness to experience the pain, shame, guilt, mortification and trauma of realizing the madness in which we ourselves have been complicit. Most people simply choose to distract themselves and avoid dealing with this most uncomfortable realization, choosing instead to stay asleep, which of course just feeds into the collective madness. Until we recognize our part in the collective madness, we have fallen prey to it and are literally supporting it by our unawareness of it.[84]

It is now beyond dispute that climate change itself affects our mental health and in fact makes the world more violent.[85] The effects of global warming, economic collapse, and the dissolution of the systems that hold industrial civilization in place will devastate the human psyche beyond anything we can imagine, and therefore, we must be skilled in living resiliently. But our resilience must not be focused only on survival. It must be transformational, not merely stabilizing.

To recognize our madness is to "befriend the dark emotions," and to open our hearts to our grief, anger, fear, and despair. In fact, we are incapable of seeing our madness or the madness of the culture and our complicity in it unless we are committed to the journey of emotional healing and shadow work and unless we have a robust bulwark of support for doing that work.

Thus, in writing this book, we wish to emphasize that the very first step in living resiliently is a commitment to the inward journey alongside our activism in the world. Inner work and activism in the world travel together and need each other. Nowhere is the inextricable connection between inner work and activism depicted more beautifully than in the 2017 VICE TV channel series, "Rise Up," in which VICE TV traveled to a number of Native American communities including those involved in the Standing Rock protests to meet people protecting their homelands and rising up against colonization.[86] Overwhelmingly, tribal activists expressed the connection between their activism and their spiritual traditions, many stating they had no idea that their activism would stir so deeply their emotional wounding and the scars of colonization such as addiction, domestic violence, and sexual abuse.

What is more, non-native activists, those who have been colonized in other ways by industrial civilization, must adopt an indigenous perspective which demonstrates reconnection in action, that is, reconnection with the sacred inner wisdom, with others, and with Earth.

The Indigenous Perspective

While there is no one "correct" indigenous perspective, our ancient past gives us clues as to how to live our future. When Andrew went to Ladakh in his late twenties, he saw a culture unstained and uncorrupted by Western consumerism, living in grounded joy and in wise harmony with nature and rooted in a simple and fervent faith in Tibetan Buddhism. This convinced him that the original face of humanity was one of great simplicity and harmony and that people could live in harsh conditions with real stability if they were attuned to nature. In his fifties, he spent a great deal of time with the Aborigines in Australia and developed a dear friendship with one of their most revered spiritual leaders, Bob Randall.[87]

In Bob's culture, everything is governed by the principle of *kanyini*, which means reciprocal relationship between human beings and animals—between human beings and nature. This was the foundation of 150,000 years of relatively peaceful living in his community.

We believe that when industrial civilization has fully collapsed, the key to resilience will be the indigenous ways. One of the most eloquent, wise, and comprehensive modern visions of this way is articulated by Oren Lyons in an address he gave to the United Nations in 1977, and it bears profound contemplation:

> Power is not manifested in the human being. True power is in the Creator. If we continue to destroy the source of our lives, then our children will suffer ... I must warn you that the Creator made us all equal with one

another. And not only human beings, but all life is equal.

The equality of our life is what you must understand and the principles by which you must continue on behalf of the future of this world. Economics and technology may assist you, but they will also destroy you if you do not use the principles of equality. Profit and loss mean nothing to future generations...

I do not see a delegation for the four footed. I see no seat for the eagles. We forget and we consider ourselves superior, but we are after all a mere part of the Creation.

We must continue to understand where we are. We stand between the mountain and the ant, somewhere and there only, as part and parcel of the Creation. It is our responsibility, since we have been given the minds to take care of these things.

The elements and the animals and the birds, they live in a state of grace. They are absolute, they can do no wrong. It is only we, the two-leggeds, that can do this.

And when we do this to our brothers, to our own brothers, we do the worst in the eyes of the Creator. [88]

Despite the horrors that have been visited on indigenous

people through colonialism and capitalist expansion, their traditions, improbably and almost miraculously, are still very alive in this moment of profound danger. We owe a boundless debt of gratitude to the sages and shamans of indigenous traditions for all they have endured to make this possible. This is all the more remarkable given the extensive capitulation of the later patriarchal, religious, and mystical traditions to the bottom-line fundamentalism of corporate culture.

Throughout the 1990s, Carolyn was profoundly influenced by the close relationship she developed with the Hopi people in northern Arizona. The suffering of the people was palpable to her and broke her heart repeatedly while at the same time, she was healed and inspired by their humor, humility, and tenacity in reclaiming their traditions and their land from the encroachment of the non-Hopi influences that surround them.

In opening to the indigenous perspective in its myriad forms that we now believe is the oxygen of survival itself, we need to be humbly and reverently respectful of each of the traditions we encounter and of the rituals of respect and courtesy that enshrine every indigenous tradition. Frequently, non-indigenous people disrespect the boundaries of indigenous communities and "borrow" from those traditions indiscriminately without permission or the blessing of indigenous elders. As well-intentioned non-indigenous individuals, we must nevertheless exercise discernment and deference in adopting indigenous rituals so that we are not inadvertently repeating the colonization pattern.

Radical Embodiment

In *New Self, New World*, Philip Shepherd writes that, "The rupture between thinking and Being is the primary wound of our culture."[89] Notice that Shepherd does not state the primary rupture is between thinking and feeling but between thinking and *Being*. He states that male energy is all about doing, while female energy is about being. While being can be defined in numerous ways, we can simplify here by asserting that being has a great deal to do with *being present*. Conscious presence in the body, with another person, with Earth, or with any situation is a direct entrance into the presence of the sacred, allowing it to touch the heart and inform the body and mind with respect to action that we may or may not need to take.

We treasure Philip Shepherd's work because we have learned much about being present in our bodies, and while our industrially civilized culture has colonized our bodies and forced us to be estranged from them, we utilize Philip's tools and share them whenever possible in our work in order to assist ourselves and others in discovering radical embodiment.

Whereas our culture has taught us that the center of consciousness is in the head, *New Self, New World* argues that the "mindful center of Being" is in the pelvis. Thus Philip speaks of "pelvic intelligence" and writes that "We are, in a literal sense all numbskulls, and it is by retreating into the skull's numbness—by 'living in our heads'—that we enter the simpler, more orderly and predictable world of doing."[90]

We highly recommend specific practices for experiencing

radical embodiment such as Qigong, Yoga, Tai Chi, and the numerous embodiment exercises available at Philip Shepherd's website www.philipshepherd.com. Along with reading *New Self, New World*, we urge you to explore and utilize these exercises, not all of which are contained in his book, in addition to any other body practices with which you are already engaged.

Embracing Simplicity and Uncertainty

The time to drastically simplify our lives is long overdue. As part of our own de-colonization, we must detoxify from consumerist culture. This does not mean that we must buy a homestead and live off-grid in a remote area. What is most urgent is to start freeing ourselves from the chains of consumerist culture in order to begin to savor a more simple existence and its rewards of leisure, silence, and space for attending to our inner journey and external service in the world.

In a culture of narcissistic entitlement and staggering abundance, the tendency to embrace an individualistic or survivalist perspective is compelling. While writing this book, we encountered numerous news stories about billionaires buying up land and creating "doomsteads," preparing to hunker down for the apocalypse. In a January, 2017 story, we notice that "The Super-Rich Are Preparing for the End of the World," and learn the extent to which they are attempting to disaster-proof their lives in advance of what they already sense will be the collapse of industrial civilization.[91]

We believe it is important to rid ourselves of the

individualistic, survivalist ethic. First of all, we should not assume that we will physically survive anything. All living beings on Earth are facing potential extinction. It is as if we are now living in a kind of planetary hospice condition in which we do not know the outcome and have very little control over it. Thus, we can be greatly served and emboldened by the words of those who embrace Buddhist teachings with regard to uncertainty. Notable examples are Jane Hirshfield, Bernie Glassman, Pema Chodron, Zhiwa Woodbury, and the late Stephen Levine. In this way we are thrust into the paradox of forging resilient lives while at the same time living as if each day may be our last. Indeed, each day *may* be our last, *and* we must live it with passion, surrender, curiosity, and a commitment to demonstrating love in action.

Community

Individualism and isolation are two aspects of what has created our predicament. Inherent in colonization is the notion of separation. We cannot overemphasize the reality that resilience is impossible without reconnection. As we navigate the global crisis in its myriad forms, we desperately need each other.

Andrew was born in India and spent time in the slums of Mumbai and Calcutta which, heartbreaking though they are, gave him hope because of the depth of cooperation between people who have nothing. Even in situations of extreme poverty, people often retain their dignity and their desire to help one another. He also lived for four years in a log cabin near rural farmers in Arkansas, and he was amazed at the cooperation he witnessed among them.

As we constantly encounter individuals who are waking up to the crisis, the most frequent complaint we hear is hunger for community. In our colonized, civilized state, we find ourselves longing for connection with others, yet so often we are alone in what we know so many others cannot allow themselves to know. And often, when we do connect deeply with allies who are astutely aware of the global crisis, we find ourselves almost needing to "re-learn" how to create and maintain the connection.

Frequently, individuals who live in or have lived in intentional communities tell us that emotional intimacy is so difficult for members of industrial civilization that in those communities, significant amounts of time are devoted to processing the emotional issues that arise from simply living together.

Yet working with the challenges of relating harmoniously with others can profoundly open our hearts and expand our capacity for demonstrating compassion, patience, and going beyond the individualism imposed by colonization. What if we find ourselves living in a dramatically impoverished, polluted, chaotic world in which all of the systems that hold society in place have collapsed? What if we find ourselves surrounded by violence and wounded, hostile, suspicious people who find it nearly impossible to trust anyone? What if we find ourselves in the midst of a pandemic or a natural disaster in which most individuals around us are sick, injured, or even psychotic? Like Andrew, we may find ourselves in a kind of Mumbai or Calcutta in which we are called to demonstrate love in action even when we have no idea how we will do so. Our one hope of staying sane and focused on service will depend on how skillfully we have evolved our community.

Sacred Relationship/Sacred Friendship

We believe that the key to resilience is sacred relationship. When we speak of relationship, we are speaking of what Andrew Harvey and Chris Saade name "evolutionary love" in their 2017 book, *Evolutionary Love Relationships*. From romantic couples to intimate family connections, friendships, and advanced professional partnerships—all can be enriched and empowered as catalysts for spiritual evolution and the transformation of consciousness. Every human relationship can be both a teacher and an opportunity to serve for the people engaged in that relationship. In fact, if the participants in the relationship view it as evolutionary in this manner, the relationship becomes a sacred adventure.

In *Evolutionary Love Relationships*, Andrew states that, "What is really at stake is this: If we continue to have a vision of relationship as purely personal, purely private, and something that we cultivate only for our own pleasure, we will keep feeding the tragic narcissism that is now ravaging the planet on every level. The real thrust and purpose and meaning and divine importance of relationship is to give us the fuel to take on the world, the passion to embrace the struggle for justice, the energy to keep on pouring ourselves out for the creation of a new world."[92]

An evolutionary relationship helps us become intensely practical, take responsibility for our behavior, and enact our sacred purpose with a partner or friend, and do so for the world. For this to happen, there are seven requirements:

1. Both beings need to be plunged individually into a deep and passionate devotion to the sacred. It must be a relationship that is undertaken in the conscious presence of the divine, for the divine's great work in the universe. Only a relationship based in the sacred will be able to bear the vicissitudes of authentic love, of dealing with the challenges of life and service in the world.

2. Both beings must develop a mastery of solitude. As Rilke wrote, "Authentic love is where two solitudes border, protect, and salute each other."[93] They border with and have boundaries and respect each other's solitude. In a true evolutionary relationship, what can exhilarate one person the most is the other's solitude because they know that solitude has the potential to make them a billionaire of generosity, of insight, and of creativity.

3. In a true evolutionary relationship there is an equality of power which is born out of a profound experience of the sacredness and dignity of the other person's soul. Andrew and Chris Saade name this as the "beloved-beloved relationship." Again, these seven requirements apply not only to relationships between romantic partners and spouses, but between friends and associates as well.

4. The relationship must be centered in the sacred. It is necessary to be master of one's own solitude so that the relationship of each person with the

divine is deepened. Sacred practices of prayer and meditation must be brought into the core of one's life so that the relationship can be enfolded in a mutually shared sacred enterprise.

5. As love becomes more evolutionary and conscious, so does each person's understanding of their own and the other's shadow. One of the essential roles in any sacred relationship is to make each person in the relationship a safe-guarder of the other's shadow. Each person must recognize where the other has been wounded and safeguard and protect them with unconditional compassion without allowing themselves to be mauled or manipulated by the other. It takes immense effort to understand one's own shadow, and an even greater effort to face and comprehend, without illusion, denial or repulsion, the shadow of the other.

6. If you are going to enter an evolutionary process, you have to accept that it never ends and never stops unfolding. Evolution is fundamentally a death/rebirth cycle that repeats itself in higher and higher dimensions. Any authentic evolutionary relationship must have the courage to go through the deaths that engender the rebirths.

7. No evolutionary relationship is exclusively private. You must engage consciously in this relationship to make you stronger, to serve the planet, to recognize that it is a relationship not only grounded in the sacred, not only infused by sacred practices, but that it is dedicated to making both people more powerful, more reflective, more passionately

> engaged with the only serious truth of our time:
> *The world is dying, and we need a major revolution
> of the heart to empower everyone to step forward and
> start doing the work of reconstruction and re-creation
> that is now desperately needed.*

In her marvelous book *World as Lover, World as Self,* Joanna Macy teaches the Four Sublime States of Buddhism: Lovingkindness, compassion, sharing joy, and equanimity. In her workshops she often incorporates an exercise in which participants walk around the room, as if they were on a crowded street or in an airport, and eventually connect with one other person, making eye contact and taking both hands in theirs. They are then guided by the facilitator in practicing one of the Four Sublime States with that person. They then move on to practice another state with another person, until all four states have been practiced with four different people.

We believe that in any relationship—between friends, lovers, associates—individuals must continue to address interpersonal and shadow issues in order to practice and live evolutionary love. Practicing the Four Sublime States allows two people to be deeply present with each other in a fashion that transcends in the moment the barriers of personal wounding and cultural conditioning. This practice is not a magic bullet that precludes addressing these, but rather, facilitates such rigorous inner work.

The Shadow in Relationships

In *Dark Gold: The Human Shadow and the Global Crisis*, Carolyn honors the voice of Jungian analyst, Robert

Johnson who wrote in his book, *Owning Your Shadow*, "Any repair of our fractured world must start with individuals who have the insight and courage to own their shadow. . . . The tendency to see one's shadow 'out there' in one's neighbor or in another race or culture is the most dangerous aspect of the modern psyche."[94]

We cannot be resilient, nor can we resist injustice without shadow healing. Doing shadow work helps us transcend a sense of "righteousness" and also gives us empathy for the oppressor. "Empathy for the oppressor," writes Miki Kashtan, "calls for an integration of self at a higher level. . . It is excruciating for any of us to realize that with different birth or social circumstances, our group could be engaging in atrocities just as easily as another group now oppressing our own."[95]

Not only does shadow healing enhance empathy, it facilitates harmonious and non-violent interaction with others and minimizes our projections not only on those we perceive as adversaries, but those we perceive as allies. Activist groups, intentional communities, humanitarian organizations, and other benevolent endeavors are often wracked with conflict because people are not attending to the shadow. They project it onto the other, dividing groups and often bringing them to total and complete demise.

Shadow work also protects us against the feel-good, delusional allurement of the New Age movement and other spiritual teachings that bypass the heartbreak of our predicament and offer the soporifics of positive thinking and narcissistic navel-gazing rather than profound inner work.

While the rational mind and ego tell us that shadow work will weaken our resilience, in fact, the opposite is true.

Making conscious our shadow material frees up enormous energy that empowers us to resist oppression and to live resiliently with compassion, open-heartedness, and a more realistic assessment of our gifts, as well as our limitations.

Relationship with Animals

In her beautiful book, *Animal Wisdom*, veterinarian Linda Bender notes that the root word of animal, *anima*, means "soul," which suggests that our reconnection with animals is a journey of renewing our own hearts and souls.[96] "The primary symptom," Bender writes, "of movement away from Paradise has been a growing estrangement from our fellow creatures."[97] According to Bender, what we do to animals, we do to ourselves. Because of our belief in their inferiority, we have infected ourselves with an inferiority complex. What we do for them, we do for ourselves. Humans and animals have a mutual need for each other: They need us to protect them, and we need them in order to make us feel happier.

From the "use" relationship inculcated with our colonization by industrial civilization, we have come to believe that like all other aspects of nature, animals exist for our consumption, pleasure, and amusement. Our perception of animals has evolved dramatically since the Enlightenment. The philosophers and scientists of that age, such as René Descartes, maintained "that animals cannot reason and do not feel pain; animals are living organic creatures, but they are automata, like mechanical robots."[98] In fact, Descartes performed ghastly experiments on animals arguing that, ". . . the exploitation of animals cannot be a wrong, for you cannot harm things, like robots or sacks of potatoes, which do not possess thoughts, feelings or a sense pain."[99]

In the twenty-first century, we now understand both scientifically and emotionally that animals not only feel pain because they are *not* mechanical robots, we also have discovered the power of one-to-one relationships with animals to bring healing calm and comfort to humans who have been severely traumatized. Increasingly, treatment programs for combat veterans suffering from Post-Traumatic Stress Disorder are experimenting with the use of service dogs. The results are significant, and often dramatic:

> At the end of 2014, the preliminary results of a year-long study of 75 such veterans conducted by Kaiser Permanente were disseminated to the public and communicated to lawmakers. The Pairing Assistance-Dogs with Soldiers (PAWS) study revealed that service dogs can "significantly reduce symptoms of post-traumatic [stress] . . . and depression in veterans." Veterans paired with service dogs reported lower symptoms of PTSD, lower symptoms of depression-related functioning, better interpersonal relationships, less substance abuse, and fewer psychiatric symptoms than veterans without dogs.[100]

A 2012 *Smithsonian* magazine article, "How Dogs Can Help Veterans Overcome PTSD," noted that "The animals draw out even the most isolated personality, and having to praise the animals helps traumatized veterans overcome emotional numbness. Teaching the dogs service commands develops a patient's ability to communicate, to be assertive but not aggressive, a distinction some struggle with. The dogs can also assuage the hypervigilance common in vets with PTSD. Some participants report they finally got some sleep knowing that a naturally alert soul was standing watch. Researchers are accumulating evidence that bonding with dogs has biological effects, such as elevated levels of the hormone oxytocin. 'Oxytocin improves trust, the ability to interpret facial expressions, the overcoming of paranoia and other pro-social effects—the opposite of PTSD symptoms,' says Meg Daley Olmert of Baltimore, who works for a program called Warrior Canine Connection."[101]

A 2012 Massachusetts Department of Correction study indicates a number of benefits resulting from prisoners working in dog training programs while incarcerated, including improved interpersonal relationships among inmates and decreased recidivism rates.[102] Further studies suggest dog training by prison inmates is not only positively affecting rehabilitation but recidivism rates as well:

> *The Pontiac Tribune* in Michigan reports that the nationwide recidivism rate hovers around 50 percent. However, Leader Dogs for the Blind, which pairs future service dogs with inmates, has a recidivism rate of just 11 to 13 percent.
>
> Only four of 35 inmates who completed one Georgia dog training program and were released have returned; without the program, coordinator Robert Brooks estimates the number would have been about 17. "It's really made an impact because guys get in here and they get attached to the animal," Brooks said.

"There is someone else counting on them to make good decisions." A *Nevada Law Journal* article on a dog training program in Washington explained that the average three-year recidivism rate in the state is 28 percent, but it is only 5 percent for inmates who have participated in the program.[103]

In our book *Return to Joy*, we noted the heroic work of animal rescuers such as Linda Tucker of the White Lion Trust in South Africa and Tia Maria Torres of the Villalobos Rescue Center in New Orleans, Louisiana. Not all of us can be world-renowned animal rescuers, but we can all do everything in our power to alleviate the suffering of animals. We can alleviate the hardships they face with the potential extinction of all species, and in the process, we can allow them to become our spiritual teachers.

What can our relationships with animals teach us? Linda Bender summarizes this beautifully:

> If we are open to it, an even deeper rapport becomes possible. We can come to share their thoughts, feelings, and perceptions, to look at the world through their eyes and see what they find so good about it. In this way, animals can become our spiritual teachers. Animals have taught me to perceive the connectedness of all living things and to experience for myself the joy they experience in this connectedness. They have taught me to accept the limits of my own understanding and to relax into the mystery of existence. They have taught me how to be less afraid of death, and less afraid of all the other

things that are not under my control. They have taught me how to lighten up and enjoy the present moment. Most of all, they have taught me how to find repose in the certainty that I am loved.[104]

Resilience and the Mother

In *Radical Passion*, Andrew wrote that any spiritual vision that does not ask us to face the appalling facts of our predicament is conspiring in our infantalization and therefore, our destruction. We are frequently asked if we are optimistic or pessimistic about the future. In fact, we believe that both optimism and pessimism are luxuries that we can no longer afford. The only response we find honorable is that of dedicated love. Whatever happens, whatever horror or destruction unfurls upon the world, however terrible the suffering of human beings and nature becomes, such a response keeps the heart open and keeps courage and compassion alive.

This response of dedicated, committed love, of love in action, springs directly from the sacred heart of the divine Mother—the Mother of the cosmos and the Mother in us. She comes to humankind in many forms: that of Kali, as the aboriginal animal the wallaby, as the sacred mystery of the Tao, and as Mary and a restored Christ. She comes as the Black Madonna and the Virgin of Guadalupe. Because we need all the help we can get, we must call on the myriad forms of the Sacred Feminine.

As we embrace the Sacred Feminine, we must also embrace the Five Sacred Passions of the divine Mother which draw from, enthuse, infuse, strengthen, sustain, and inter-illuminate each other. Lived together in every dimension for Her and in Her, they represent the full alchemical force of divine human love in reality.

1) *The First Sacred Passion:* The passion for the Source, the Transcendent, fuels all the others. While it is true that the patriarchal bias toward transcendence has resulted in a destructive rejection of women, nature, and the body, it is also true that contemporary overemphasis on the Immanent can cut us off from those sources of transforming power that are the gift of the invisible and Transcendent. To be in continual, loving contact with the Transcendent is vital for the stamina and illumined wisdom we need to survive. All of the Mother-mystics make clear that we come to know that nature is entirely holy and in fact *is* Her body. "God's grandeur," Gerard Manley Hopkins writes, "will flame out from shook foil."[105] Nature *is* that "shook foil" from which the grandeur of the divine Mother is continually and incessantly flashing, if the eyes of love are open in us. From this immanent knowledge of Her splendor in every fern and dolphin and wave and rose and deer and hippopotamus and orchid and windswept sand dune arises, then, the Second Sacred Passion.

2) *The Second Sacred Passion:* The passion for nature is the passion for the source of all created things and for the humility of the source's presence in and as all things. St. Francis of Assisi talked with sparrows, wolves, snakes, turtledoves, and all the

elements as his brothers and sisters, as equals. As mentioned above when we focused on the topic of reconnection, we cannot be connected only with self and other because we not only issue from Earth, but we *are* Earth. We are not *part of* Earth or *in harmony with* Earth; we *are* Earth. Disconnected as we have been from Earth, it may require months, years, or even the rest of our lives to grasp that we are Earth and feel in our bodies what that actually means. Earth is not only the Mother's body; it is our body as well, and whatever destruction is visited upon Earth is also visited upon our own bodies. Likewise, any care and kindness bestowed upon the body of Earth is bestowed on all living beings.

3) *The Third Sacred Passion*: The sacred passion for all sentient and human beings—the passion of the bodhisattva, of those who deeply understand our *interbeing* with all being, our total and fundamental interconnectedness with everyone and everything in the entire cosmos. In fact, *in*dependence does not exist in nature. Rather, we are profoundly *inter*dependent and interconnected with all living beings. We are implicated in every life and every death, in every injustice, in every crime, in every casual, premeditated, or unconscious brutality. On the one hand, this may feel terrifying to contemplate because it shows us that there is no escape anywhere from this tremendous responsibility of love. Yet we cannot be genuinely resilient unless we are attuned to the divine Mother, and our felt sense of interdependence makes that attunement possible.

4) *The Fourth Sacred Passion*: The Fourth Sacred Passion is a passion for the mysterious force of the Mother's unified field that enables the union of all opposites—the union of body and soul, the union of masculine and feminine, the union of races, ethnicities, countries, and spiritual traditions in a common vision of a sacred world and a sacred humanity.

5) *The Fifth Sacred Passion*: The Fifth Sacred Passion prevents all other passions from becoming decadent, narcissistic, or escapist because the Fifth Sacred Passion is the passion for service and love in action. Daring to allow the fire of the Mother into our lives is daring our lives to burn away in that fire, to be transformed continually to reflect ever more richly and intensely the Mother's laws of love and justice.

Every sea must be cleaned for Her, every ravaged forest restored, every endangered species—including those parts of the human population facing a kind of selective genocide—protected, every commercial arrangement that threatens the creation in any way forbidden. The force of the Mother is a revolutionary force of love that works incessantly to break down *all* barriers and separations in the name of love; it hungers to see *this* world become the stable paradise it already is in Her mind of truth. Unless we serve that force and will and strive to put into living practice its unsparingly radical injunctions, we are not loving the Mother but a watered down, personally tailored version of Her that can only keep us trapped in illusion, and the world trapped in its headlong rush toward annihilation.

The revolution of the Mother demands of each of us unstinting service. What does such service mean? It means dedicating our every gift and power, our every prayer, our every thought and emotion and perception, to the welfare of others in the world. It means having the courage and patience to learn all the dreadful facts about what is happening and how we—all of us—conspire in what is happening. It means taking *personal* political responsibility on local, national, and global levels, alone and together. It means scrutinizing who we vote for, who we give power to, and holding them to their promise of change for as long as we have the freedom to do so. It means realizing, once and for all, with no false consolation of any kind, in just what terrible danger we are and how each of us will have to dedicate our entire being and intelligence to focused, thoughtful acts of loving service to all, if we are going to have any chance of surviving.

The service the Mother is asking of us in this catastrophe is as humble, supple, many-faceted, loyal, indefatigable, and extreme as hers. And when these Five Sacred Passions live in us and we in them, then we will be living the full human-divine life in the Mother. We will be awake in Her Sacred Heart, living and acting from it, and with its blessing and serving power.

Humor

On January 19, 2017, comedian and host of the television show, "Full Frontal," Samantha Bee, interviewed activist and author, Masha Gessen, who grew up in the Soviet Union and now lives in the United States. In the interview entitled, "Samantha Bee and Masha Gessen Discuss Why

Panic Is the Best Form of Resistance on 'Full Frontal',"
Gessen states that with the inauguration of Trump, we are
staring into an abyss, and democracy is unlikely to return to
us anytime soon. In her own inimitable way, Samantha sets
up the interview in a dark, quiet room off a noisy gym where
people are frantically riding stationery bikes. She begins by
asking Gessen questions about autocratic regimes. With
each naïve question to Gessen about what will happen under
a Trump administration, the stoic Gessen takes Samantha
farther down a rabbit hole of despair, quoting an old Russian
saying, "We thought we had hit rock bottom, and then
someone knocked from below.[106] The brilliantly crafted
interview leaves us chuckling at Samantha and imagining
how a conversation between Franz Kafka and Mary Poppins
might have looked. And although we are laughing, another
part of us recognizes the terrifying reality through which
Gessen has lived and which she coldly relates to the nearly
clueless Samantha.

For months after the 2016 election, American culture
was buoyed by *Saturday Night Live* skits depicting Donald
Trump, played by Alec Baldwin, and other cast members
playing characters such as Vladimir Putin, Kellyanne
Conway, Sean Spicer, and a variety of political personalities.
While Donald Trump was frantically tweeting disparagingly
in protest of the skits, millions of Americans' sides were
splitting with laughter. As this book enters publication, it
appears that the White House is now mired in scandal.
Sean Spicer has resigned from his position as White House
Press Secretary, and Reince Preibus has been replaced as
White House Chief of Staff by former Homeland Security
Secretary, General John Kelly. Some media have described

the current White House as a circular firing squad and as the most dysfunctional White House in recent memory.

A recent headline on the Raw Story website proclaims, "We Have Melissa McCarthy to Thank for Sean Spicer's Downfall—Raising His Profile Was the Kiss of Death."[107] This after many months of McCarthy impersonating Sean Spicer providing daily White House press briefings. While the outrageous chaos in which the White House is currently engulfed and which promises to become even more preposterous is ultimately dangerous and deplorable, many Americans are taking comfort in humor in order to endure the spectacle.

Thus, late-night comedic geniuses including Stephen Colbert, John Oliver, Trevor Noah, and Jimmy Fallon create a groundswell of resistance through humor which not only speaks truth to power but does so in a manner that mesmerizes American culture. At the same time, comedy genuinely offers relief by sending a message that even in the madness of Trump's victory, clarity and decency still have a subversive voice and so make the reality of a Trump presidency less paralyzing.

In turbulent and trying times, humor can be personally and culturally therapeutic, even in the most brutal situations. In fact, according to the Holocaust Teacher Resource Center, Jews during the holocaust kept sadness and depression at bay by using humor. Chaya Ostrower in "Humor as a Defense Mechanism in the Holocaust," investigates humor and laughter in the holocaust and the functions they fulfilled. Even in Auschwitz, Jews shared humorous stories and jokes in order to maintain their sanity.[108] Victor Frankl noted in *Man's Search for Meaning* that, "Humor was another of the soul's weapons in the fight for self-preservation. It is well known that humor, more than anything else in the human makeup, can afford an aloofness and an ability to rise above any situation, even if only for a few seconds."[109]

Throughout human history, in times of oppression people have not only found solace in humor, but resisted oppression with satire, sarcasm, slapstick, dark humor, self-deprecating humor, and using humor to bond with each other.

Redefining Hope

We would like to distinguish between authentic hope and lazy hope. Lazy hope is the indulgence in what people imagine to be hope without any conscious commitment to transforming the structures that are destroying our world. It frequently cohabits with bland, magical thinking that assumes we will be looked after no matter what we do. Authentic hope is a direction of the entire being toward a transformed future, fused with relentless commitment to working towards that future.

Portland vocalist and composer, Barbara Ford, sings her beautiful, compelling song, "Hope Is What You Do (Not What You Have)" In publicizing her work, Ford writes:

> Hope is what we do, not something we have. In reclaiming hope as a stance and an embodied intention, we free ourselves to choose how we will live with integrity, no matter the circumstances. The ongoing work for justice calls us to grow our capacities to resist the messaging of consumer culture, oppression,

> powerlessness, and polarization. We are
> also called to strengthen our personal and
> collective capacity for connection, creativity,
> and commitment to ourselves and the larger
> world community.[110]

Similarly, Rebecca Solnit writes that "Hope is not a lottery ticket you can sit on the sofa and clutch, feeling lucky. It is an axe you break down doors with in an emergency. Hope should shove you out the door, because it will take everything you have to steer the future away from endless war, from the annihilation of the earth's treasures and the grinding down of the poor and marginal. . . . To hope is to give yourself to the future—and that commitment to the future is what makes the present inhabitable."[111]

In *Active Hope: How to Face the Mess We're in Without Going Crazy*, Joanna Macy and Chris Johnstone explain that:

> Active Hope is a practice. Like tai chi or
> gardening, it is something we *do* rather than
> *have*. It is a process we can apply to any situation,
> and it involves three key steps. First, we take a
> clear view of reality; second, we identify what
> we hope for in terms of the direction we'd like
> things to move in or the values we'd like to see
> expressed; and third, we take steps to move
> ourselves or our situation in that direction.
>
> Since Active Hope doesn't require our optimism,
> we can apply it even in areas where we feel
> hopeless. The guiding impetus is intention; we
> *choose* what we aim to bring about, act for, or
> express. Rather than weighing our chances and

proceeding only when we feel hopeful, we focus
on our intention and let it be our guide. [112]

As Andrew emphasizes in *The Hope: A Guide to Sacred Activism*, we must avoid the triumphalist mentality and be open to the outcome of our efforts, not determined to control them. As Carolyn writes in her article "When Surrender Means Not Giving Up,"[113] the sacred inspiration we require results not from lazy hope or finding solutions, but from a state of active being in which we voluntarily enroll in radical psychological and spiritual training. If we haven't registered for this psycho-spiritual apprenticeship, then we will persevere in our triumphalist agenda and inadvertently perpetuate despair.

Activist Miki Kashtan writes that "Non-attachment is not about letting go of wanting. Rather it's about owning our needs and staying open to the possibility of having them continue to be unmet, which is and has been the reality for so many of us for so many centuries or more." We bring our hearts into our work and talk less about what "must" happen and more about the pain at what *is* happening and our longing for a different world.[114]

Kashtan explains that letting go of attachment is not the same as letting go of our desire for change. For example, we want all of the children of the world to be safe and have sufficient food. We work toward that end. Rather it is about being able to tolerate internally the possibility that it might not happen that all of the children in the world will be safe and have sufficient food. "If we cannot tolerate this possibility—which is also the current reality!—then how can we have space inside to interact with life as it is?"[115]

Sacred inspiration, sacred practices, and spiritual training which includes shadow work—these give us the capacity to accept life as it is and not force a "solution" while working tirelessly with un-illusioned, rugged hope toward a more just world. The greatest Sacred Activists have always understood that their dreams will not be completely realized in their lifetimes, yet this has never stopped them from giving everything they are and have to birth the possibilities they know can help heal and transform human experience.

Suggested Practices

** Journal topic: When did I last experience awe? What was that like? What happens to me when I experience awe?

** Journal topic: When did I last experience beauty? What feels beautiful to me? Commit to experiencing at least five minutes of beauty today—through visual art, music, nature, and more.

**Regularly engage in embodiment practices such as Yoga, Tai Chi, Chi Gong. Become familiar with the work of Philip Shepherd, author of *New Self, New World* and a variety of embodiment exercises available for downloading at his website. Whether using Philip's book or downloading from his website, learn and practice the Wakame Exercise[116] frequently—one of the most powerful and pleasurable exercises for experiencing resilience in the body. Thinking about resilience and actually feeling it in the body are two different realities.

**Journal or draw or express in an art form your relationship with one or more animals in your life. How did the animal(s) break your heart open? What was your relationship with it/them like? How was this animal(s) a spiritual teacher for you? Is there a particular way of serving animals that calls you at this time?

**Take one-half hour or longer to journal about a time in your life when you were forced to make a sudden change such as suddenly losing a job or suddenly being forced to move your residence or needing to adapt to some unforeseen, unwelcome situation. How did you respond to the situation? In what ways did you react from an ungrounded condition of panic? In what ways did you respond from a more grounded place of intention and moving forward? Do not judge either response as good or bad, but notice what served you and what did not.

Chapter 4

Regeneration: The Legacy of Love in Action

Most of the great victories continue to unfold, unfinished in the sense that they are not yet fully realized, but also in the sense that they continue to spread influence. A phenomenon like the civil rights movement creates a vocabulary and a toolbox for social change used around the globe, so that its effects far outstrip its goals and specific achievements—and failures. [117]
—Rebecca Solnit, *Hope in the Dark*

Oh very young, what will you leave us this time?
—Cat Stevens, 1974

At a summer conference in 2013, Carolyn met a young man who was a student at the University of Kentucky, and who asked her to come to his community and offer a weekend workshop. She was somewhat taken aback that a university student was aware of her work and was inviting her to speak to his peers. It was the beginning of a sweet connection between Carolyn and Tyler Hess, who three years after his graduation calls himself a regenerative farmer and who is committed not only to organic farming, but to mastering herbal medicine and gourmet natural food cooking. Tyler shared his vision in a podcast with Carolyn in 2017.[118]

In 2015, Carolyn met Erica Martenson from western Massachusetts, who in her early twenties had chosen, after a couple of years of community college study, to focus on growing food and learning land and resource stewardship skills. In 2016, Erica was a guest on Carolyn's podcast, *The New Lifeboat Hour.* When Carolyn asked her what she would like to say to older generations, Erica replied that she would like baby boomers to take some responsibility for squandering resources and creating climate catastrophe. One way they could do this is by investing parts of their nest egg, if they have one, into positive changes in the world, particularly in protecting and stewarding land. In addition, they can share the skills they have acquired throughout their lives. What the world needs, Erica says, is not more elderly tourists, but elders who take responsibility for their actions and attempt in every way to create a better world.[119] In other words, elders can claim their role as elders and understand that growing older is not synonymous with becoming an elder.

Elderhood is not a state of aging but rather, a state of consciousness—an attitude that one assumes willingly. In his delightful book, *Elders Rock: Don't Just Become Older, Become an Elder,* Harvey Austin, MD defines elderhood as, "the stage of wisdom, compassion, and joy—life in full bloom. Elders have gained a profound understanding of the world as it is. They are the reservoir of both the secular and the spiritual history of our species, and they use their knowledge for the good of all. Their longer view allows Elders to see the patterns of life clearly and to look down the path for many generations."[120]

What octogenarian Harvey Austin implies in this statement is that elderhood is much more about wisdom than it is about age. Certainly, life experience is relevant, but we all know individuals in their eighties and nineties who have remained children in terms of wisdom, and we all know twenty- and thirty-year-olds, such as Tyler and Erica, who are wise beyond their years.

Michael Meade in *Fate and Destiny* beautifully clarifies this distinction:

> Experience alone does not add up to genuine wisdom. Wisdom combines life experience with insight into oneself and into the world. Those who would become elder and wiser learn to extract living knowledge from the specific dramas and struggles, the tragedies and comedies they experience in life. . . The elders carry a greater vision of life because they develop insight into their own lives.[121]

We have observed and experienced that a commitment to deep inner work, including shadow work, and a heartfelt commitment to a spiritual path, are invaluable assets for developing a capacity to "extract living knowledge" from the vicissitudes of our human existence.

While we were writing this book, Harvey Austin shared with us a beautiful article by his friend, Julian Spalding, in which the author states:

Clearly, from our limited human perspective, we are witnessing the beginning of the death throes of industrial civilization. This is cataclysmic, beyond human ability to fully comprehend. What does this mean for our way of life? How will we survive? Will we survive? Maybe a better question is who will we be together in the face of this unprecedented challenge of our time? I doubt if we will emerge the same people we are now. Industrial man may not be able to survive in the new world. The Gene Keys [by Richard Rudd] states, "A new network of neuro-circuitry in the solar plexus is superseding the reptilian fear-based neuro-circuitry of the old brain." If this is true, then we may be literally evolving a New Human Operating System.[122]

In other words, Spalding argues that nature knows what she is doing as humans have created a trajectory toward extinction for many, perhaps all species on Earth. In fact, he dares to ask the question, "Is it possible we are the culmination of a vast experiment of a vast intelligence we can barely fathom from our limited human intelligence? Is it possible that our very disconnection from "Nature" is actually Her intent?"[123]

We do not believe that Spalding's theory justifies settling back into some literal or symbolic La-Z-Boy recliner and giving up. Rather, we must first of all stay open to the possibility that within one hundred years or much sooner, few life forms will remain on Earth. With this possibility in mind, we must focus on the overarching task of regeneration, that is, creating a legacy of love in action.

Regeneration's Imperative

In *The Direct Path*, Andrew offers a host of practices for creating a personal journey to divine consciousness. He completes the book with a firm reminder that one's spiritual path is not undertaken merely for personal fulfillment or ecstasy or the accumulation of amazing powers, but rather, for service: Service to the divine, to one's own self, service to family and friends, service to the community, service to the world and all living beings.

1.   We serve the divine through our spiritual practices such as meditation, ritual, the study of sacred texts, and artistic expression which may enrich the lives of others but which above all, honor the sacred. We are reminded that at the end of all of his church compositions, Johann Sebastian Bach wrote the initials, "S.D.G." which stood for "Soli Deo gloria," or "Glory to God alone."

2.   Service to the divine leads naturally to service to the Sacred Self. This does not mean that we become "self-serving," but rather, recognizing the difference between the Sacred Self within us and the culturally-conditioned ego self, we honor both our humanity and our divinity by caring for ourselves physically and emotionally. We honor the body by practicing a healthy lifestyle which includes rest, healthy eating, and the cultivation of embodiment as noted in our references to the work of Philip Shepherd. We strongly encourage our readers to download and study Philip's Embodiment Manifesto[124] and

to become familiar with his work. One of the most important ways of serving oneself is to become fully present in the body because if we are not, it is nearly impossible to serve ourselves or anyone else.

3. When we serve the divine and ourselves, we naturally want to serve our family and friends. Often we are asked by individuals who have awakened to the global crisis and find it difficult to discuss their thoughts and feelings about it with family and friends, what they should do. Our answer: Love them—love them with all your heart and soul, even if they never share your perspective on our planetary predicament. Serve the animal members of your family and allow them to love you and teach you their wisdom.

4. Be aware of what is happening in your community and find ways to serve it through volunteering in a hospice facility, a nursing home, a homeless shelter or soup kitchen, an animal shelter, or some other entity that serves the community. Humans are starving for a sense of belonging and community, and engaging with others in service for your town or village is a beautiful way to experience the first major concept of this book: Reconnection.

5. One can serve the world in numerous ways. One of the most important is to simply be informed of current and world events. We are particularly shocked when spiritual seekers tell us that they do not read the newspapers or access news on the internet, radio, or television. To stay informed is an important service to the world. For this reason, in

2007, Carolyn created a subscription-based Daily News Digest that offers news on issues of economics, the environment, geopolitical issues, civil liberties and human rights, and culture. At the end of each Digest is an Inspiration section which contains a number of news stories highlighting ways in which various individuals and communities are addressing the global crisis. If you are able, contribute with your money and time to organizations that are addressing the global crisis and creating a better world.[125]

Blogger and financial writer Charles Hugh Smith in a 2017 post entitled, "Millennials Are Homesteading, Buying Affordable Homes, Building Community," notes that "While it's certainly good sport to mock 'snowflakes,' not all Millennials are snowflakes. Many are homesteading, buying affordable homes and building communities that get stuff done." Smith relates the story of millennial, Drew Sample:

> Although the mainstream media focuses on bubble-priced Left and Right coast homes costing hundreds of thousands of dollars, there are perfectly serviceable houses that can be had for $50,000 or less elsewhere in America. Drew just bought one, and rather than go through a bank for the mortgage, he arranged (with the help of a real estate attorney) for a family member to put up the mortgage.
>
> This arrangement is win-win: the family member earns a much higher return on the cash than a savings account or equivalent, the

loan is secured by the property, and Drew cuts out the bank/lender.

It may surprise those who only read media accounts of Millennials living in their parents' basement playing videogames that many of the Millennials in Drew's "tribe" are growing food via homesteading.[126]

The Sanctity of Food

Few people on Earth understand the dire state of humanity's current food supply and what is likely to be severe and ultimately fatal disruptions in our food supply in the coming years due to climate chaos and industrial farming. One person who understands our food predicament more clearly than anyone we know is Michael Brownlee of Boulder, Colorado, author of *The Local Food Revolution: How Humanity Will Feed Itself in Uncertain Times*. In this book, Brownlee is inciting a local food revolution, and this revolution is far more expansive, far more radical, and far more life-altering than creating a few farmers markets and promoting one's local economy. According to Brownlee, our industrial food system "has itself become the greatest threat to humanity's being able to feed itself." However, this revolution is not merely an uprising against the global industrial food system but also a "coming together to build something new in the face of nearly impossible odds." In fact, it is a spiritual, as well as a social and political event because it will require us to learn how to feed ourselves. What is more, it is a "center of aliveness in the midst of a dying civilization" which "provides more than hope; it is a revolution of the deeper meaning and purpose and presence that lie ahead, emerging mysteriously out of a convergence of seed, soil, soul, and stars." The Unholy Alliance—Big Food, Big Ag, and Big Pharma, empowered by Big Banking and Big Government has deprived us of the autonomy of learning how to feed ourselves and has also convinced farmers, entrepreneurs, and investors that solutions for feeding the world are technological only.[127]

In other words, in the local food revolution that must happen, "we are not attempting to change or fix the global industrial food system. We're simply putting all our efforts into building our own food system, our own regional foodsheds." According to Brownlee, we must "resign as consumers" and opt out of the global food system which is what the Unholy Alliance fears most: Losing control of our food supply, but more fundamentally, losing control of us.[128]

For Brownlee, the realization that we are now facing impending catastrophic climate change has been life-changing in the way that near-death experiences often are. He notes that abrupt climate change is giving humanity a near-death experience that may provide, as such experiences often do, an entirely new outlook on life. Part of this new outlook for the author has been his countless epiphanies with regard to food and the possibility of an emerging food revolution. Such a revolution could not have occurred in the context of business as usual but rather, as Brownlee states, "the food revolution manifesting around local food can occur only at the moment of the death of a civilization . . . in the same way that the supernova process is possible only with the death of a star."[129]

Thus, urgent, radical involvement in our local food system, as well as how we prepare, cook, preserve, and conserve our food is a pivotal aspect of regeneration. Our practices for growing and distributing food in the face of catastrophic climate change and toxic industrial food policies must be solidly in place, otherwise regeneration will not be possible, because those remaining on the planet will perish.

The earliest humans were hunter-gatherers who never knew exactly where their next meal might be coming from. In fact, their "meals" were probably eaten on the run as they stalked enough prey to constitute an actual meal, but it is unlikely that their meals were regular or even eaten daily. Given the conditions under which they secured food, it was impossible for them to take any of it for granted. Every morsel was hard-won and therefore, exceedingly precious.

When humans became sedentary, they transitioned from hunting and gathering to growing their own food, and while this made eating more predictable as a result of a more stable lifestyle, few ate mindlessly. Whether living in a small agricultural village along the Nile River in ancient times or growing food in one's backyard garden in the twenty-first century, small-scale agriculture is labor-intensive, and appreciation for food is greatly enhanced by the energy expended in growing it.

Sedentary societies were dependent on the kindness of nature to provide the rain and sunshine necessary for growing food. Thus, many Earth-based forms of spirituality evolved in which humans experienced a direct connection between the agricultural harvest and a particular deity such as Osiris in Egypt and Ceres in Rome. As part of their gratitude for what they believed the deity had provided, people offered food to the gods and goddesses of nature.

Throughout human history, particularly in indigenous cultures, food has been perceived as sacred. The word *sacred* is not a religious term but rather one that simply means "set apart" or not of the ordinary. It is also related to "sacrifice," which may mean that something is sacred because it derived from something sacrificed. For example, we speak of battlefields and military cemeteries as sacred. In ancient times, some temples, mountains, or forests were sacred because animals were sacrificed to a god in those places. All food is sacred in the sense that the life of a plant or animal has been sacrificed to feed another being.

Ancient, traditional societies understood that food is life force energy for which they needed to exert significant amounts of energy, whether by hunting or growing it in order to eat. Because their survival was often in jeopardy, food became sacred to these cultures.

With the mass movement of people from the land to cities, the sanctity of food was eclipsed by fascination with artificial, synthetic, and technologically-produced forms of food. No longer was it necessary to hunt or grow food because now it was delivered from short or long distances to nearby markets. Thus it seems that the sacredness of food decreased in proportion to the energy required to obtain it.

At this moment we are witnessing, and many of us are participating in, an unprecedented transition from industrial agriculture to sustainable (local, organic) agriculture. While this transition has been shaped by declining resources, including fossil fuels, and while an increasing number of individuals prefer to eat foods grown closer to home that have not been contaminated with pesticides, attempting to define the transition exclusively in terms of science or sustainability discounts the role of the human soul in it. In other words, there is a spiritual component to this phenomenon.

In his article "Reclaiming the Sacred in Food and Farming," Emeritus Professor of Agriculture and Economics, John Ikerd of the University of Missouri writes of the spirituality of sustainable agriculture and asks, "What is this thing called spirituality?" His answer: "[S]pirituality is not religion, at least not as it is used here. Religion is simply one of many possible means of expressing one's spirituality. William James, a religious philosopher, defined religion as 'an attempt to be in harmony with an unseen order of things.' Paraphrasing James, one might define spirituality as 'a need to be in harmony with an unseen order.' This definition embraces a wide range of cultural beliefs, philosophies, and religions."[130]

Ikerd proceeds to quote statements defining spirituality from a variety of cultures, but he summarizes them by saying:

> A common thread of all these expressions of spirituality is the existence of an unseen order or interconnected web that defines the oneness of all things within a unified whole. We as people are a part of this whole. We may attempt to understand it and even influence it, but we did not create nor can we control it. Thus, we must seek peace through harmony within the order of things beyond our control. This harmony may be defined as "doing the right

things." And, by "doing the right things" for ourselves, for others around us, and for those of future generations, we create harmony and find inner peace.[131]

As students of mythology and ritual, we must also ask what the symbolism of this transition may be for our time. On some level, whether conscious or unconscious, we are all aware of the dire predicament in which we and our planet are mired at this point in human history. In fact, we believe that through a return to sustainable agriculture and in the very act of growing our own food, some aspect of the human psyche is bowing to the Earth and the sacred in gratitude for and resonance with the elements of the soil from which we have evolved. The ramifications of this in our lives and our communities have been and may well continue to be astounding—a renewed reverence for the Earth, a heightened appreciation for nutrition and the health benefits of organic food, a deepened connection with our families and communities around growing and eating food in our local place, and enmeshing local foodsheds directly with local economic development to name only a few.

The opposite of the sacred, of course, is the profane. Something in our ancient memory understands that mindlessly-manufactured and technologically-tortured so-called "food" constitutes the most profane of substances which are unfit to be ingested in human bodies. The more deeply immersed we are in the sanctity of food and its origins, the more we are likely to be repelled by processed, genetically modified, and chemically-laden foods that have been produced by way of massive resource and ecological destruction, and which deliver more of the same to our physiology.

The sacred within us instinctively resonates with the sanctity of food. Therefore, the growing, transporting, distribution, and consumption of food are sacred acts that deserve ritual and reverence from the moment the seed is planted in the Earth to the moment we have washed and put away the plate on which our food was served.

How then specifically do we respond when we return to the reality of food as sacred? Peter Bolland in his article, "The Sacrament of Food" says, "Maybe the most sacred space in your home is not the yoga room, or the altar with the candle, or the chair by the window where you meditate and pray. Maybe the most sacred room in your house is the kitchen." But our interaction with food begins far in advance of preparing it in the kitchen. Here are some suggestions for cultivating more mindful reverence in our relationship with food:

- Know exactly where your food comes from. Read labels, ask questions, and research sources for whole, organic foods in your region.
- Consider becoming a community supported agriculture (CSA) member. This allows you to buy directly from the farmer or grower.
- Give thanks when you shop—thank the food you purchase, thank the market staff, and give thanks that you can afford to shop.
- Commit to purchasing 10% or more of your food that is grown locally.

- Mindfully plan your meals. Perhaps it won't be possible for you to eat at home today or tomorrow or the next day because you are traveling or because of time constraints. Plan a strategy for eating in places where nourishing food is served or plan to bring healthy snacks with you.

- Take a moment or two to stop before eating and give thanks for your food. Remember to thank the people who grew, harvested, transported, and distributed your food. Thank plants and animals for their lives and the sacrifice they made with their lives so that you can be fed.

- Regularly enjoy food with family and friends. Cook and eat meals together. Share the sacrament of food with each other in potlucks or other gatherings.

- Occasionally share extra food or leftovers with neighbors or people who are not in your family or circle of friends. In a world of skyrocketing food prices and climate change, food "security" may become increasingly "insecure," and sharing food with others communicates a subtle message that you are concerned about their well-being in hard times. Reaching out in this way encourages reciprocity around food so that when someone has little or no food, others are more motivated to share.[132]

While eating is a political and an economic act, it is also a sacrament. How we eat matters not only to ourselves but to everyone else, or in the words of Peter Bolland, "The way we eat is the way we live. How we eat is who we are. Let us affirm that which is best in us and in each other through the sacrament of food."[133]

A Prayer to Future Beings

For decades, Joanna Macy has cherished and shared a vision of awakening to our predicament and catalyzing planetary healing which she names the Work That Reconnects during this time which she calls the Great Turning. Of this she writes, "The central purpose of the Work That Reconnects is to help people uncover and experience their innate connections with each other and with the systemic, self-healing powers in the web of life, so that they may be enlivened and motivated to play their part in creating a sustainable civilization."[134]

As we have emphasized throughout this book, reconnection with self, other, and the Earth is humanity's core mission at this moment, regardless of the fate of the planet. We cannot meaningfully engage in resistance, fine-tune resilience, or expedite regeneration unless we are willing to commit to the heartbreaking, heart-opening work of reconnection.

We offer Joanna's prayer for future beings:

You live inside us, beings of the future.

In the spiral ribbons of our cells, you are here. In our rage for the burning forests, the poisoned fields, the oil-drowned seals, you are here. You beat in our hearts through late-night meetings. You accompany us to clear-cuts and toxic dumps

*and the halls of the lawmakers. It is you who drive
our dogged labors to save what is left.*

*O you who will walk this Earth when we are
gone, stir us awake. Behold through our eyes the
beauty of this world. Let us feel your breath in our
lungs, your cry in our throat. Let us see you in the
poor, the homeless, the sick. Haunt us with your
hunger, hound us with your claims, that we may
honor the life that links us.*

*You have as yet no faces we can see, no names
we can say. But we need only hold you in our
mind, and you teach us patience. You attune us
to measures of time where healing can happen,
where soil and souls can mend. You reveal courage
within us we had not suspected, love we had not
owned.*

*O you who come after, help us remember: we are
your ancestors. Fill us with gladness for the work
that must be done.*[135]

Suggested Practices

**Return to the first paragraphs of this chapter and the
vision of millennials, Tyler Hess and Erica Martenson. What
do you feel as you read about the path they have chosen for
their future? [Links to the podcasts with Tyler and with
Erica may be found in the Endnotes section of this book.]

How does their vision inspire you?

**Re-read the words of Harvey Austin earlier in this chapter regarding elders. What is your understanding of the true definition of an elder? Ponder the difference between "older" and "elder." Journal your insights.

**The local food revolution, permaculture, and organic agriculture are only a few examples of regenerative practices. What are some others? Regardless of our chronological age, we are all ancestors. If we do not recognize that role, then it is waiting for us to claim. What legacy are you committed to leaving for those who may outlive you?

**In your journal, take plenty of time to write a prayer for future beings. Allowing yourself to feel how dangerous and daunting their future is likely to be, move deeply into your heart and beyond good wishes for "safety, peace, and prosperity." Know that your prayer for them is also a prayer for yourself, and in that tender, vulnerable knowing, write or speak your prayer.

Chapter 5

Celebrating Reconnection, Resistance, Resilience, and Regeneration

Only in the hall of praise should lamentation go.
—Rainer Maria Rilke, *Sonnets to Orpheus*

Centuries before words like "the collapse of industrial civilization" or "global crisis" were being articulated by humans, ancient prophecies predicted our current collective experience.

In North America, elders of the Hopi tribe spoke of "The End of the Fourth World." Although the prophecies had been a part of Hopi oral tradition for centuries, the elders began making them public shortly before the mid-twentieth century. Researcher Gary David notes that:

> Like the Maya, among whom the Hopi once lived and with whom they later traded, the Hopi conceptualize the cycles of time as world-ages. The Hopi believe that we have suffered three previous world cataclysms. The First World was destroyed by fire—a comet, asteroid strike, or a number of volcanic eruptions. The

Second World was destroyed by ice—a great Ice Age. As recorded by many cultures around the globe, a tremendous deluge destroyed the Third World. These three global destructions were not the result of merely random earth changes or astrophysical phenomena but of humankind's disregard both for Mother Earth and for the spiritual dictates of the Creator. In other words, cataclysmic events in the natural world are causally connected to collective transgressions, or negatives human actions.[136]

Hopi elders assert that we are now living in the Fourth World, and when these cataclysmic events begin to occur, humans will have a choice to follow the true path of wisdom or go the "zig-zag way." Some of the cataclysmic events they have predicted which Gary David notes are:

[T]he possibility of the Fourth World's demise. These involve an increasingly erratic climate and a few specific signals or signs of social and political imbalance. The prophesized Earth changes include earthquakes, tsunamis, hurricanes, tornadoes, record flooding, wildfires, droughts, and famines. Pandemics are currently on the minds of many. The 2014 Ebola virus epidemic in West Africa claimed over 5,000 victims as of the end of October, 2014. The U.S. Centers for Disease Control and Prevention projected as many as 1.4 million fatalities by January of 2015.

The Hopi also predicted a number of technological changes that would signal the end of the Fourth World. Long before it happened, the elders said a "gourd of ashes" would fall on the Earth. This refers, of course, to nuclear explosions—first the atomic test blast at Trinity Site in New Mexico, then the dual holocausts at Hiroshima and Nagasaki, and finally the other hydrogen bomb tests on Pacific atolls and in the American Southwest (with their carcinogenic effects on the "down-winders"). Hopi prophecies include the fact that people would ride in "horseless wagons" on "black ribbons" (vehicles on asphalt). In addition, aerial vehicles would travel "roads in the heavens" (pathways in the sky, either benign contrails or deleterious "chemtrails"). The Hopi also stated that one of the final signs is that people would be "living in the sky" (International Space Station).

According to David, we must remember that "Hopi prophecies are not contemporary readings of world events, but statements made centuries or perhaps millennia ago. These disturbing commentaries on our current state of global affairs were simply relayed through the generations to the present via the Hopi oral tradition, with very few alterations made in the process."[137]

Likewise, the Kogi people living in the Sierras of Colombia declare that:

> The sacred sites of the indigenous peoples of the world form a network of spiritual communication around the globe. As these sacred sites are destroyed, and as the people

who have cared for these sites are removed and assimilated, this communication network has been broken. The spiritual fabric of the Earth has been torn to shreds and the people who hold the ceremonies that keep the Earth in balance cannot correct things anymore. The non-native nations, who the Four Tribes of La Sierra call "little brother," are out of control and have gone too far. It is too late for us, as humans, to correct this on our own. If we do not re-activate the sacred sites and re-activate the higher beings who can help us restore order to the world, we will not be able to re-weave the spiritual fabric of the Earth. The mother is crying. She is weeping for her children. She is in pain, and will speak with her voice of wind, water and fire . . . louder and louder . . . unless we begin to speak for her and do what she is asking.[138]

According to Eco Watch online, "The Tribes of the Sierra have begun a unification process for the awareness of the life originating principles, called IKWASHENDWNA, which is the urgent call to internal order that the Mother makes to humanity. It is a call for all peoples to unite in the efforts to stop "little brother" in his plunder. We must also unite in our efforts to return the sacred sites to their original guardians, so that the proper ceremonies can be carried out and the activations can be completed. We must continue to march, to speak, to be active ourselves . . . but without the help of the higher beings we are tilting at the windmills of destruction that we ourselves have created."[139]

In addition to the Hopi and Kogi prophecies, the

prophecies of Nostradamus, Edgar Cayce, the Aztecs, and the Maya conjecture a time of chaos, a cataclysm for the Earth and its inhabitants. And of course, as noted at the beginning of this book, Hindu tradition speaks of the Kali Yuga, which many believe we have entered.

As we awaken to this variety of indigenous prophecies regarding the demise or unraveling of human civilization on this planet, and if we take them seriously as we live amid what appears to be the fulfillment of them, how will we respond? How will we respond in a manner that embraces and lives *Reconnection, Resistance, Resilience,* and *Regeneration?*

In this book, we have endeavored to offer a fundamental structure for responding, along with specific tools for doing so. Another perspective that summarizes this structure is offered by Linda Tucker, founder of the White Lion Trust in South Africa. Linda offers a specific training for learning *LionHearted Leadership* in the face of the current unraveling. She states that symbolically, lions always represent leadership. Moreover, there are two forms of leadership that have taken place in humankind's history: self-service and serving the greater good. In her leadership training course, Linda offers 13 Laws of *LionHearted Leadership*[140]:

1) *Origination: Follow your paw print*: Being original means being your true self and embarking on your own unique journey which means also being prepared to honor those who came before you. Yet while all of us are unique and special, the shadow sides of Origination might be a sense of superiority which could subtly lead us to what Tucker calls the

Tyrant Approach or a belief in inferiority which could lead to a Victim Approach. As she writes, "Origination is a journey of self-discovery that makes life worth living, no matter the challenges."[141]

2) *Appreciation: Celebrate your nature*: This requires genuine gratitude and thanksgiving in every given moment. To give thanks supports our Lion Hearts and supports others to reconnect with their Lion Hearts. The shadow sides of this law might be overindulgence or taking more than your fair share or conversely, failing to employ gratitude due to fear and insecurity.

3) *Communication: Share the roar*: This law requires us not only to speak out but to listen—listen at a heart-to-heart level. A lion communicates loudly, boldly, and with absolute authority. Yet while roaring, it is important to deliver the message in a tactful and appropriate way. The shadow sides of the Law of Communication might be invasion or communicating in an insensitive, controlling, or invasive way. The opposite may happen if we fail to communicate intimately, honestly, and from our hearts. Often this results from the fear of giving ourselves, the fear of sharing, listening, and actually learning—or simply not being fully present.

4) *Nurturance: Encourage fresh growth:* Just as we attend to blossoming and developing our own lives, we must foster growth in others. An important piece of nurturance is developing a sense of your own home space. The LionHearted leader attends to growth

within herself as well as constantly encouraging fresh growth in others. The shadow side of Nurturance may be either turning Nurturance into personal gain at the expense of others or stifling and curbing the flourishing we see in others.

5) *Radiance: Protect the LionHeart:* Tucker argues that given the stress of our modern life, it is impossible to enact *LionHearted Leadership* without specific embodiment practices. Fuller embodiment promotes radiance---allowing ourselves to shine as we let go of the need for approval. It means connecting our own heart with the heart of creation. It allows our true light to shine---the light we see in the faces of Nelson Mandela, the Dalai Lama, and Jane Goodall. This radiance gives us "solar power" to stand up for what we believe, and we become Love personified. One shadow side of radiance might be over-exposure or the desire to always be seen or on the other hand, fear of exposure stemming from fear of criticism or judgment. Examples of people who abuse and exploit their charismatic light are everywhere. We need not be one of them, nor need we shrink from allowing our radiance to be seen and felt.

6) *Regeneration: Serving Mother Earth:* This law is in direct conflict with the heroic, consumeristic mindset instilled in us by industrial civilization. Among other blessings, the Sixth Law teaches us how to deal with failure. We cannot call ourselves leaders unless we are serving Earth. As with the other Laws, shadow sides exist. We might seek

to exploit this law for personal gain or without regard to the whole ecosystem. "Playing God" with resources such as genetic engineering or artificial intelligence do not serve Mother Earth. Likewise, becoming paralyzed or apathetic and doing nothing leads to profound degeneration in our lives and the deterioration of our health.

7) *Collaboration: Find your pride:* This is the Law of relationship and inter-relationship. A true leader *acts in service of and connection with others.* "Pride" in *LionHearted Leadership* terms "is the recognition of self-worth and value in others, including their achievements."[142] Finding our pride means that we cannot be leaders without doing so in connection and collaboration with others through shared empowerment. Groupthink or a mob mentality is one of the shadow sides of this Law. Cults, ethnic separatism, and a mob mentality or "in-crowd" exclusivity do not foster collaboration. Nor does the opposite shadow so pervasive throughout industrial civilization: narcissism. Self-centeredness and arrogance have no place in the pride whose purpose is to support all members in surviving and thriving.

8) *Authentication: Gain full responsibility: LionHearted Leadership* requires a deeply responsible approach to life. Yet our responsibility is a gift and does not have to be a burden. This law defines our relationship with power—whether we use it skillfully or abuse it. Tucker writes that: "Responsibility comes *before* power. We become empowered precisely because we *have* taken up and shouldered responsibilities for the

greater good, as opposed to self-serving leadership which seizes power without gaining responsibility or being held responsible." [143] One shadow side of Authentication might be the authoritarian position of assuming that one is the final authority whereas the opposite manifestation of the shadow might be that of shirking responsibility and blaming others.

9) *Co-creation: Live your dreams:* This law requires us to "align our heart's dream with the creative Source itself and thereby draw on the ultimate power."[144] Aligning our will with the divine will, may be uncertain at best and terrifying at worst. Yet we do this in order to have the potential to co-create something or many things that may be beyond our wildest dreams. One shadow manifestation of this Law might be manipulation if we attempt to exploit the Law for personal gain. Disbelief and doubt are manifestations of the opposite shadow.

10) *Governance: Steward your resources:* With this law it is essential to establish a clean and clear relationship with money. We must expand our definition of resources beyond the material perspective and "manufactured money," to "the true values of reflecting humanity's ability for loving creativity and co-creativity." Tucker notes that white lions are apex predators which means that they take only what they need, and like other apex predators, restore balance all the way down the food chain in an ecosystem. If we want to know the health of an ecosystem, we need to look at the health of the apex predator. One shadow side of the Law

of Governance is dominion, again misusing a Law for personal gain. The other side may be the mismanagement and squandering of resources and gifts, including the unique, personal gifts we came here to give--which the next Law addresses.

11) *Liberation: Uncage your gifts:* We must celebrate not only our own gifts but the gifts of others. By respecting the gifts of others and joining our own gifts with theirs, we have the potential of revitalizing life and creating joy. One shadow approach leads us to control the gifts of others and upstage our own or conversely, we may fail to recognize our own gifts and become passive-aggressive, self-pitying, or want to be rescued.

12) *Aspiration: Rediscover the stars:* Utilizing this Law, we make connections with greater causes. This Law reminds us that "the purpose of our time here is for humans to evolve spiritually, and find our unique place and path to higher consciousness...." All of nature is our teacher offering lessons of wisdom for our illumination and that of all humanity. Yet it is important that we remain grounded and embodied in doing so and that we are not drifting into the territory of spiritual bypassing. On the one hand, we might be tempted to de-motivate and demoralize others in their pursuit of their dreams, or we might have given up on our dreams and cower in shame or resentment.

13) *Elimination: Cleanse your kingdom:* Discernment or knowing what to discard or eliminate from

your life and path is essential to leadership. It is important to constantly "spring clean" and de-clutter and clear out dead matter so that new and vital energy can come in. On one shadow side, the furthest extreme would be killing, exterminating, and making extinct. On the other side, we might fail to remove that which is harming the body or the ecosystem. We may succumb to inertia, stagnation, and contamination---physical, mental, or spiritual.

Progress in employing the laws is not linear but rather moves in a spiral fashion. They provide a set of exquisite practices to keep our hearts, minds, and bodies fine-tuned and enhance our commitment to living resiliently. We believe that living the principles of *LionHearted Leadership* is essential as we endeavor to practice *Reconnection, Resistance, Resilience*, and *Regeneration*.

Celebration and Imagination

In addition, we assert that in order to realize and live the "Four Rs" of the dark night of the globe, we must infuse our lives and our work with celebration. Without it, these words remain only concepts in our minds rather than the lifeblood of our being. The word *celebrate* means to "honor, solemnize, laud, glorify, honor, applaud, commend."[145] What then is it that we are to celebrate in a time when celebration may seem like the most unlikely response to our predicament?

We believe that ritual, imagination, and spiritual values must be celebrated alongside our passionate activism and that our celebration must be as vital as our resistance. Yet ritual, imagination and spiritual values do not originate from the intellect, but issue from suffering as Jungian analyst Marion Woodman, speaking about the American psyche, asserts:

> When a culture doesn't make room for ritual and imagination, and if spiritual values are taken out of the center of the culture, then what is left? And if there is no genuine suffering taking place at the soul level [of the culture], then the music is not new; the ballet is not new; the theater is not new.

> And if there is no ritual that people believe in— and ritual in this context means undergoing a [psychological or spiritual] death, a period of being in the dark hole of chaos, followed by a rebirth—then people don't truly grow up. In a ritualistic society, for example, young people really believe that during their culture's coming-of-age rites, they may die. Through these rituals they have to prove that they are strong enough and mature enough to enter the adult world, which also means they have to know and understand the culture they are moving into. The older people educate them about their culture by telling them stories. Well, who's interested in stories in our culture? So you see, the culture itself, from my point of view, is no longer organic. And once the culture fails, civilization fails.

> But I also believe that there is a new global culture being called for—and that means that

every country is going to have to surrender its selfish nationalism and open up to a global community. The earth has moved from tribe to group to country and then to international trade laws and international connection—and now even these systems are too small. We are moving towards global community, and in the process narrow [nationalistic] loyalties will have to be surrendered to the larger whole.[146]

It is crucial that we allow Woodman's words to sink in: *And if there is no ritual that people believe in—and ritual in this context means undergoing a [psychological or spiritual] death, a period of being in the dark hole of chaos, followed by a rebirth—then people don't truly grow up.*

Only suffering can compel humanity to embrace the path of *Reconnection, Resistance, Resilience,* and *Regeneration* and to commit to *LionHearted Leadership* and the celebration not only of spiritual values but of the regeneration that we are endeavoring to bring to fruition. For years, we have argued that humans are experiencing a planetary rite of passage or initiation by way of the global crisis. It is compelling us to surrender to an initiatory ordeal in which we are forced to descend into the dark night of the globe collectively and the dark night of the soul individually so that the transformation of collective and individual consciousness may occur, for as Carl Jung insisted, "There is no coming to consciousness without pain."[147]

We cannot end this book responsibly without pointing out that we may, and sooner than we think, find ourselves in a terminal situation. By now, we hope we have made clear that we if we come to such a situation, *Reconnection,*

Resistance, Resilience, and *Regeneration* will all be as sacred and important, if not more so, than they are now. How will we endure the end of everything we hold dear without being grounded in the deathless truth of the Sacred Self and of each other and of Earth? How will we stay human if we do not continue, even in the face of overwhelming oppression and violence, to resist in large and small ways with the full force of our souls? How will we not shipwreck on the rocks of paralysis and despair if we do not learn now the laws and tools of resilience? And even if we are destined to disappear as the human race, won't it be our duty to try to leave the planet as intact as we possibly can for the regeneration we cannot now imagine but can pray for?

There is a great and holy secret the ancient Hindu texts concerning Kali Yuga offer us. That is, that in many paradoxical ways (and who is the queen of paradox but Kali herself?), Kali Yuga is the best age to live in for two reasons: 1) The shattering of all illusions can, if you let it reveal reality in all its terrible and amazing splendor, liberate you finally; 2) In Kali Yuga the grace pouring down to help human beings endure is greater and more resplendent than in any other age.

We have discovered for ourselves the extraordinary truth of what the Hindu sages say. The destruction of every illusion does not end in horror, paralysis, and despair. It ends in the open expanse of a love beyond reason and agenda which reveals itself burning in every flower and every grain of sand and radiating from every face. The shattering of every false hope does not end in hopelessness and the desire to die. It ends in awe at the majesty of the force and presence and omnipotence of the divine. Those of us who allow Kali to kill in us everything that is false and insincere and addicted to magical thinking will discover that the "killer goddess" is also the re-birther—the One who destroys you only to give you the incomprehensible and glorious miracle of herself.

With all that we inevitably have to face and accept, we must never forget what we all somewhere know within ourselves—that joy is the ultimate nature of reality and the fuel for all authentic survival. In the spirit of this joy, we would like to celebrate the infinite wellspring of joy that resides at our core and that cannot be destroyed by the worst agony and the most devastating defeat.

In the spirit of the Upanishads that proclaim "From joy all beings have come, by joy they all live, and unto joy they all return,"[148] we wish to conclude this book by celebrating ten things that we enduringly love:

1) Our wonderful animal companions, Sammy and Jade, without whose love our lives would be so much darker.

2) All of our friends who join us in heartbreak, hope, and joy in the adventure to help create possibility in catastrophe.

3) All of the extraordinary, brave, and precise voices in the media who radiate truth in an age that is losing its capacity to determine it: Noam Chomsky, Chris Hedges, Amy Goodman, Gary Null, Rachel Maddow, Chris Hayes, Lawrence O'Donnell, Joy Reid, Naomi Klein, Elizabeth Gilbert, Thom Hartmann, Abby Martin, and so many others.

4) The tireless work of all Sacred Activists everywhere, often in terrible circumstances and with no recognition or funding. For us, you redeem the human race, and we bow to you. We honor your sacrifices and in many cases, your willingness to pay the ultimate sacrifice. May we be worthy of you.

5) The great composers, artists, and mystical poets of all cultures who keep the flame of divine passion burning in our long night.

6) The blessed, holy comedians who keep outrageous truth and freedom alive.

7) The great world teachers such as His Holiness the Dalai Lama, Jane Goodall, Desmond Tutu, Joanna Macy, and Matthew Fox, who show us how to live in joy whatever happens. They never stop loving and pouring themselves out.

8) The great mystical classics such as the Upanishads, St. John's Gospel, the Gospel of Thomas, the Song of Songs, the Zohar, the Bhagavad Gita, the Koran, and others from all traditions that remind us of our origin and our essential identity. Their inspiration is needed more now than ever.

9) The great transpersonal psychologists who have done such heroic work in helping us see, heal, and integrate the shadow and begin the work of uniting body and soul. These include Carl Jung, Francis Weller, Meg Pierce, Nathan Schwartz-Salant, Marion Woodman, Clarissa Pinkola Estes.

10) Forever and always, the divine Mother in whom we place all of our passionate desires for *Reconnection, Resistance, Resilience,* and *Regeneration.* May your mercy and infinite love save us from ourselves. May we grow strong and wise enough to be worthy of your Savage Grace.

Of all the words with which we could leave you, these sublime truths that St. John of the Cross expresses with matchless clarity are the ones that move us the most:

> *The eternal fountain is unseen*
> *in living bread that gives us being*
> *in black of night.*
> *She calls on all mankind to start*
> *to drink her water, though in dark,*
> *for black is night.*
> *O living fountain that I crave,*
> *in bread of life I see her flame*
> *in black of night.*

About the Authors

Andrew Harvey, author of 30 books, is Founder Director of the Institute for Sacred Activism, an international organization focused on inviting concerned people to take up the challenge of our contemporary global crises by becoming inspired, effective, and practical agents of institutional and systemic change, in order to create peace and sustainability. Sacred Activism is a transforming force of compassion-in-action that is born of a fusion of deep spiritual knowledge, courage, love, and passion, with wise radical action in the world. The large-scale practice of Sacred Activism can become an essential force for preserving and healing the planet and its inhabitants. His work can be explored in depth at www.andrewharvey.net

Carolyn Baker is the author of *Love in the Age of Ecological Apocalypse: The Relationships We Need to Thrive* (2015) as well as *Collapsing Consciously: Transformative Truths for Turbulent Times* (2013). Her

previous books are *Navigating the Coming Chaos: A Handbook for Inner Transition* (2011) and *Sacred Demise: Walking the Spiritual Path of Industrial Civilization's Collapse* (2009). In 2016 she published *Dark Gold: The Human Shadow and the Global Crisis.* She lives and writes in Boulder, Colorado, and manages her website www.carolynbaker.net. A former psychotherapist and professor of psychology and history, Carolyn is a life coach and consultant for people who want to live more resiliently in the present as they prepare for the future. Her podcast, the New Lifeboat Hour airs regularly online.

Endnotes

1   "Alternative Facts: A Psychiatrist's Guide to Twisted Relationships to Truth," Ronald Pies, The Conversation, March 1, 2017, http://theconversation.com/alternative-facts-a-psychiatrists-guide-to-twisted-relationships-to-truth-72469

2   "Lie to Me: Fiction in the Post-Truth Era," Adam Kirsch, *New York Times*, January 15, 2017, https://www.nytimes.com/2017/01/15/books/lie-to-me-fiction-in-the-post-truth-era.html?_r=0

3   "Czeslaw Milosz's Battle For Truth," Adam Kirsch, New Yorker, May 29, 2017, http://www.newyorker.com/magazine/2017/05/29/czeslaw-miloszs-battle-for-truth

4   "The Dark Night of the Soul," Eckhart Tolle, https://www.eckharttolle.com/newsletter/october-2011

5   William Blake, *The Four Zoas*, Create Space, 2015, p.49.

6   "Why Uncertainty Can Cause Stress," Liji Thomas, M.D., Medical Net News, http://www.news-medical.net/health/Why-can-Uncertainty-Cause-Stress.aspx

7   Jamie Holmes, *Nonsense: The Power of Not Knowing*, Broadway Books, 2015, p. 9.

8   Ibid., p.15.

9   Ibid., p.12.

10 Andrew Harvey, *The Essential Mystics*, Holy Quar'an, Surah 6, Harper One, 1997, p140.

11 "Remembering Stanley Kunitz," by Jane Hirshfield, author of "Uncertainty," https://www.poetryfoundation.org/features/articles/detail/68569

12 Andrew Harvey, *The Hope: A Guide to Sacred Activism*, Hay House, 2009.

13 Margaret Wheatley, "Who Do We Choose to Be?" http://margaretwheatley.com/wp-content/uploads/2017/05/MW-WhoDoWeChooseToBe.pdf

14 Marion Woodman: *Dancing in the Flames: The Dark Goddess in the Transformation of Consciousness*, Shambhala, 1997, p.139.

15 "Kali Takes America: I'm With Her," Vera de Chalambert, *Rebelle Society* blog http://www.rebellesociety.com/2016/11/18/veradechalambert-kali/

16 Ibid.

17 Ibid.

18 "The Serpent and the Dove: Wisdom for Navigating the Future," by Andrew Harvey and Carolyn Baker, http://www.huffingtonpost.com/entry/the-serpent-and-the-dove-wisdom-for-navigating-the_us_58335fbfe4b0eaa5f14d4963

19 Urging Millions to Rise Up, Trump Foes Issue Call to 'Resist Fascism', http://www.commondreams.org/news/2017/01/04/urging-millions-rise-trump-foes-issue-call-resist-fascism

20 Ana Navarro: It's hard to give Trump a chance when he staffs his White House with racists, http://www.rawstory.com/2016/11/ana-navarro-its-hard-to-give-trump-a-chance-when-he-staffs-his-white-house-with-racists/

21 Dave Chapelle, Saturday Night Live, November 13, 2016, https://www.youtube.com/watch?v=--IS0XiNdpk

22 Carolyn Baker and Stephen Jenkinson, The Lifeboat Hour, August 28, 2015, https://soundcloud.com/orphan-wisdom/stephen-jenkinson-lifeboat-interview-with-carolyn-baker

23 Miriam Greenspan, *Healing Through the Dark Emotions*, http://www.miriamgreenspan.com/excerpts/introEx.html

24 Carolyn Baker, *Navigating the Coming Chaos: A Handbook for Inner Transition*, iUniverse, 2011, p. 81.

25 Coleman Barks, *The Essential Rumi*, Castle Books, 1997, p. 36.

26 Naomi Klein, *No Is Not Enough: Resisting Trump's Shock Politics And Winning The World We Need,* Haymarket Books, 2017, p.13.

27 Ibid., p.23.

28 Ronald Reagan Inaugural Address, University of California, Santa Barbara, http://www.presidency.ucsb.edu/ws/?pid=43130

29 Ibid., p26.

30 Carl Jung, *The Collected Works*, "Psychology and Alchemy," Part II, CW 12, p. 221

31 "Our Part In The Darkness," Rabih Almaddine, New Yorker, Feb 5, 2017, http://www.newyorker.com/culture/culture-desk/our-part-in-the-darkness

32 Dean Walker, *The Impossible Conversation: Choosing Reconnection and Resilience at the End of Business as Usual,* Amazon Create Space, 2017.

33 Chris Hedges, "American Psychosis," *Truthdig* [January 29, 2017] http://www.truthdig.com/report/item/american_psychosis_20170129

34 Rebecca Solnit, *Hope in The Dark: Untold Histories, Wild Possibilities*, Haymarket Books, 2016, p.12.

35 Moira Weigel, "How the Right Invented a Phantom Enemy," https://www.theguardian.com/us-news/2016/nov/30/political-correctness-how-the-right-invented-phantom-enemy-donald-trump?CMP=share_btn_tw

36 Ibid.

37 Ibid.

38 Ibid.

39 Robert Paxton, *The Anatomy of Fascism*, Vintage, 2005, p. 218.

40 Eisenhower Archives, President Eisenhower's Farewell Address, 1961, https://www.eisenhower.archives.gov/all_about_ike/speeches/farewell_address.pdf

41 Greg Palast website, "The Best Democracy Money Can Buy," http://thebestdemocracymoneycanbuy.com/

42 Kali Holloway, "Trump Is an Eerily Perfect Match With a Famous 14-Point Guide to Identify Fascist Leaders," Alternet, December 6, 2016) http://www.alternet.org/election-2016/trump-eerily-perfect-match-famous-14-point-guide-identify-fascist-leaders

43 Ibid.

44 James McDougall, "No, This Isn't The 1930s, But Yes, This Is Fascism," https://theconversation.com/no-this-isnt-the-1930s-but-yes-this-is-fascism-68867

45 Peter Dreier, "American Fascist," January 20, 2017, http://www.commondreams.org/views/2017/01/20/american-fascist

46 Robert Klitzman, "Trump and a Psychiatrist's Views of Sociopathy and Narcissism." http://www.huffingtonpost.com/robert-klitzman-md/trump-a-psychiatrists-vie_b_12670806.html

47 *Washington Post,* "CNN Commentator: Scottie Nell Hughes, "Facts No Longer Exist," https://www.washingtonpost.com/blogs/erik-wemple/wp/2016/12/01/cnn-commentator-scottie-nell-hughes-facts-no-longer-exist/?utm_term=.1c9486f4fd39

48 "What Is Artificial Intelligence?" Kai Fu Lee, New York Times, June 24, 2017, https://www.nytimes.com/2017/06/24/opinion/sunday/artificial-intelligence-economic-inequality.html

49 "Blind Spot," Peter Russell, http://www.peterrussell.com/blindspot/blindspot.php

50 Ibid.

51 Ibid.

52 Nathan Schwartz-Salant, *The Order-Disorder Paradox: Understanding The Hidden Side of Change In Self and Society*, North Atlantic Books, 2017.

53 "Priebus: Trump Considering Amending or Abolishing 1st Amendment," Talking Points Memo, April 30, 2017, http://talkingpointsmemo.com/edblog/priebus-trump-considering-amending-or-abolishing-1st-amendment

54 "Trump's Russian Laundromat," Craig Unger, New Republic, July 13, 2017, https://newrepublic.com/article/143586/trumps-russian-laundromat-trump-tower-luxury-high-rises-dirty-money-international-crime-syndicate

55 Ubiquity University Blog, Jim Garrison, January 29, 2017, http://ubiquity.university/index.php/component/easyblog/make-the-earth-great-again?Itemid=280

56 "Exon Mobil Could Tap Huge Arctic Assets If US-Russia Relations Thaw," December 13, 2016, http://www.cnbc.

com/2016/12/13/exxon-mobil-could-tap-huge-arctic-assets-if-us-russian-relations-thaw.html

57   Naomi Klein, *The Shock Doctrine: The Rise of Disaster Capitalism,* Picador Publishing, 2008.

58   Derrick Jensen, "Unsettling Ourselves," https://unsettlingamerica.wordpress.com/2012/02/12/derrick-jensen-civilization-decolonization/

59   Ibid.

60   Ibid.

61   Chris Hedges, "Revolt Is the Only Barrier to a Fascist America," Speech in Washington, DC, January 21, 2017. http://www.truthdig.com/report/item/revolt_is_the_only_barrier_to_a_fascist_america_20170122

62   Chris Hedges, *The Wages of Rebellion*, Nation Books, 2016, p. 18.

63   Ibid. p. 86.

64   Website of Andrew Harvey: www.andrewharvey.net

65   *Wages of Rebellion,* p. 225.

66   "How to Build an Autocracy," David Frum, *The Atlantic,* March, 2017, https://www.theatlantic.com/magazine/archive/2017/03/how-to-build-an-autocracy/513872/

67   Ibid.

68   Ibid.

69   "Containing Trump, Jonathan Rauch, *The Atlantic,* March, 2017, https://www.theatlantic.com/magazine/archive/2017/03/containing-trump/513854/

70   Ibid.

71   Ibid.

72   "For Defeat of Trumpcare, Thank Disability Rights Activists, Not John McCain," Jake Johnson, Common Dreams, July 28, 2017, https://www.commondreams.org/news/2017/07/28/defeat-trumpcare-thank-disability-rights-activists-not-john-mccain

73   Mark Engler and Paul Engler: *This Is an Uprising: How Nonviolent Revolt Is Shaping the Twenty-First Century,* Nation Books, 2016, p. 32.

74 Ibid., p. 32.

75 Ibid., p. 194–195.

76 Ibid., p. 161.

77 Momentum Training website http://movementmastery -movementmastery.nationbuilder.com/

78 Ibid., p. 283.

79 Chris Hedges, "American Psychosis," *Truthdig*, January, 2017, http://www.truthdig.com/report/page2/ american_psychosis_20170129

80 Naomi Klein, *No Is Not Enough: Resisting Trump's Shock Politics And Winning The World We Need,p13.*

81 Ibid, p. 12.

82 Gracepoint Wellness website, Harry Mills, Ph.D., Mark Dombeck, Ph.D. http://gracepointwellness.org/298- emotional-resilience/article/5779-defining-resilience

83 Victor Frankl, *Man's Search for Meaning*, Penguin-Random House, Republished, 2014, p. 115.

84 Paul Levy, "Why Don't We See Our Collective Madness?" Awaken In the Dream website, http://www.awakeninthedream. com/why-dont-we-see-our-collective-madness/

85 "How Climate Change Makes the World More Violent," *Washington Post,* May 21, 2015, https://www.washingtonpost. com/news/monkey-cage/wp/2015/05/21/the-threat-to-security- from-climate-change-may-be-even-more-prevalent-than- previously-thought/?utm_term=.1487894c210f

86 VICE TV "Rise Up" documentary series, 2017, https://www. viceland.com/en_us/show/rise

87 Wikipedia, Bob Randall, https://en.wikipedia.org/wiki/ Bob_Randall_(Aboriginal_Australian_elder)

88 *The Essential Mystics*, Edited by Andrew Harvey, Harper One, 1997, pp.14-15.

89 Philip Shepherd. *New Self, New World*, North Atlantic Books, 2010, p. 90.

90 Ibid. p. 73.

91   CNBC, "The Super-Rich Are Preparing for the End of the World, January 25, 2017, http://www.cnbc.com/2017/01/25/the-super-rich-are-preparing-for-the-end-of-the-world.html

92   Andrew Harvey, Chris Saade, *Evolutionary Love Relationships: Passion, Authenticity, and Activism*, Enrealment Press, Toronto, Canada, 2017, p. 9.

93   Rainer Maria Rilke letter to Franz Kappus, May 4, 1904, http://www.carrothers.com/rilke7.htm

94   Robert Johnson, *Owning Your Own Shadow: Understanding the Dark Side of the Psyche*, Harper One, 1991, p.x.

95   Miki Kashtan, *Reweaving Our Human Fabric: Working Together to Create a Non-Violent Future*, Fearless Heart Publications, 2014, p.61.

96   Linda Bender, *Animal Wisdom: Learning from the Spiritual Lives of Animals*, North Atlantic Books, 2014, xvii.

97   Ibid., p. 6.

98   Animal Ethics, René Descartes, Chapter 7 http://www.animalethics.org.uk/descartes.html

99   Ibid.

100 American Medical Association Journal of Ethics, June, 2015, http://journalofethics.ama-assn.org/2015/06/hlaw1-1506.html

101 "How Dogs Can Help Veterans Overcome PTSD," *Smithsonian* magazine, July, 2012, http://www.smithsonianmag.com/science-nature/how-dogs-can-help-veterans-overcome-ptsd-137582968/

102 Prison Animal Programs: A Brief Review of the Literature, Massachusetts Department of Corrections, 2012, http://www.mass.gov/eopss/docs/doc/researchreports/prisonanimalprogramsliteraturereviewfinal.pdf

103 "Man's Best Friend: How Dog Training Is Affecting Prison Rehabilitation," Alvernia University, October, 2015, http://online.alvernia.edu/how-dog-training-is-affecting-prison-rehabilitation/

104 Linda Bender, *Animal Wisdom,* p. 15.

105 "God's Grandeur," Gerard Manley Hopkins, https://www.poetryfoundation.org/poems-and-poets/poems/detail/44395

106 "Samantha Bee and Masha Gessen Discuss Why Panic Is the Best Form of Resistance on 'Full Frontal'," http://splitsider. com/2017/01/samantha-bee-and-masha-gessen-discuss-why-panic-is-the-best-form-of-resistance-on-full-frontal/

107 "We Have Melissa McCarthy to Thank for Sean Spicer's Downfall," Raw Story, May 26, 2017, http://www.rawstory. com/2017/05/we-have-melissa-mccarthy-to-thank-for-sean-spicers-downfall-raising-his-profile-was-the-kiss-of-death/

108 Chaya Ostrower, "Humor as a Defense Mechanism in the Holocaust," https://www.yadvashem.org/yv/en/education/ conference/2004/55.pdf

109 Victor Frankl, *Man's Search for Meaning*, pp.63–64.

110 350 PDX https://350pdx.org/event/hopeiswhatyoudo/

111 Rebecca Solnit, *Hope in the Dark: Untold Histories, Wild Possibilities*, p.4.

112 "Defining Active Hope in a Changing World," Joanna Macy, Chris Johnstone, *Utne Reader,* September, 2012, http://www. utne.com/mind-and-body/active-hope-ze0z1209zsch?pageid=2 #PageContent2

113 "When Surrender Means Not Giving Up," Carolyn Baker, https://carolynbaker.net/2014/05/27/when-surrender-means-not-giving-up-the-new-sacred-activism-by-carolyn-baker/

114 Miki Kashtan, *Reweaving Our Human Fabric: Working Together to Create a Non-Violent Future,* Fearless Heart Publications, p.57.

115 Ibid., p. 58.

116 Wakame Exercise, *New Self, New World*, Philip Shepherd, https:// books.google.com/books ?id=uGLpGdspjeIC&pg=PA65& lpg=PA65&dq=Philip+Shepherd+wakame+exercise&source= bl&ots=YKp2oXOg0r&sig=tS4DAuiHmwjqJGrRookjNhU MT7Q&hl=en&sa=X&ved=0ahUKEwjTvteTl5PUAhVM-2MKHdAGCdkQ6AEIPDAE#v=onepage&q=Philip%20 Shepherd%20wakame%20exercise&f=false

117 Rebecca Solnit, *Hope in the Dark: Untold Histories, Wild Possibilities,* Haymarket Books, 2016, p.63.

118 New Lifeboat Hour, Across The Generations Between Boomer And Millennial: Navigating Endings And Beginnings At All Ages, Tyler Hess and Carolyn Baker, July, 2017, http://drumbaker.podbean.com/e/across-the-generations-between-boomer-and-millennial-navigating-endings-and-beginnings-at-all-ages/

119 The New Lifeboat Hour, Podcast, "Navigating The Global Crisis As A Millennial," Erica Martenson and Carolyn Baker October 10, 2016, https://drumbaker.podbean.com/e/navigating-the-global-crisis-as-a-millennial/

120 Harvey Austin, *Elders Rock: Don't Just Get Older, Become an Elder*, published by Harvey Austin, MD, 2015, xxii.

121 Michael Meade, *Fate and Destiny: The Two Agreements of the Soul,* Greenfire Press, 2010, p.89.

122 "Does Nature Know What She Is Doing?" by Julian Spalding, Julian Spalding Blog, https://julianspalding.wordpress.com/2016/03/07/does-nature-know-what-she-is-doing/

123 Ibid.

124 The Embodiment Manifesto, Philip Shepherd, https://philipshepherd.com/manifesto/

125 Andrew Harvey, *The Direct Path*, Broadway Books, 2000, pp. 272–273.

126 "Millennials Are Homesteading, Buying Affordable Homes, Building Community," Charles Hugh Smith, Of Two Minds Blogspot, April 13, 2017, http://www.oftwominds.com/blogapr17/millennials-halfx4-17.html

127 Michael Brownlee, *The Local Food Revolution: How Humanity Will Feed Itself in Uncertain Times*, North Atlantic Books, 2016.

128 Ibid.

129 Ibid.

130 "Reclaiming the Sacred in Food and Farming," John Ikerd, University of Missouri, http://web.missouri.edu/ikerdj/papers/Sacred.html

131 Ibid.

132 "The Sacrament of Food," Peter Bolland, http://peterbolland.blogspot.com/2012/12/the-sacrament-of-food.html

133 Ibid.

134 "A Prayer to Future Beings," Joanna Macy, http://www.joannamacy.net/prayer-to-future-beings.html

135 Ibid.

136 "Hopi Prophecy and the End of the Fourth World, Part 1," Gary David, Ancient Origins archeological research website, http://www.ancient-origins.net/myths-legends-americas/hopi-prophecy-and-end-fourth-world-part-1-002280

137 Ibid.

138 "An Urgent Message from the Kogi and the 'Living Relic'," Bethany Yarrow, EcoWatch http://www.ecowatch.com/an-urgent-message-from-the-kogi-and-the-living-relic-1881953185.html

139 Ibid.

140 Linda Tucker, *The 13 Laws of LionHearted Leadership*, Npenvu Press, 2017.

141 Ibid., p. 88.

142 Ibid., 131.

143 Ibid., 137.

144 Ibid., 143.

145 Dictionary.Com, *Celebrate*, http://www.dictionary.com/browse/celebrate?s=t

146 "Jungian Analyst Marion Woodman on the American Psyche," *Psychology Today,* May, 2017, https://www.psychologytoday.com/blog/america-the-couch/201705/jungian-analyst-marion-woodman-the-american-psyche

147 Carl G. Jung, *Contributions to Analytical Psychology*. London: Routledge & Kegan Paul, 1928, p. 193.

148 The Essential Mystics, p.37.

Made in the USA
Lexington, KY
06 June 2018